Advance praise for *Forest Church*:

Don't read this book if you're not ready to be surprised—and quite possibly delighted. Our alienation from the natural world is well documented, and Bruce Stanley offers tried-and-tested ways to rebuild our connections, whether in urban park or remote forest, with the possibility of personal renewal and even encounters with the divine along the way.
Olive Drane, author of Spirituality to Go, fellow of St. Johns College Durham, England, and affiliate professor at Fuller Theological Seminary, California

Bruce Stanley takes us on a highly readable journey out into nature to discover a new form of Church. Not only does the book remind us of nature's ability to speak powerfully about God, it also serves as an effective reminder of the urgent need to bring spiritual depth to the task of caring for the earth. I've been lucky enough to attend Bruce's Forest Church in Mid Wales where we found meaning in some of the simplest things we experience on a daily basis and yet seldom take time to ponder. Sharing this encounter with others was enriching and refreshing. I am privileged to support this venture.
Rt. Rev. Andrew John, Bishop of Bangor

Forest Church

FOREST CHURCH

A Field Guide

to a Spiritual Connection

with Nature

BRUCE STANLEY

Forest Church © Bruce Stanley, 2014

Anamchara Books
Vestal, New York 13850
www.anamcharabooks.com

First Published in the UK in March 2013 by
Mystic Christ Press
Troed Yr Esgair Barn
Llangurig
Powys, SY18 6RS

Grateful thanks go to *Third Way* magazine for giving permission to reprint
content that was originally published in the May 2012 issue.

10 9 8 7 6 5 4 3 2 1

Printed in the United States of America.

ISBN: 978-1-62524-008-8
Ebook ISBN: 978-1-62524-009-5

Typeset and design by Vestal Creative Services
Vestal, New York
www.vestalcreative.com

For Gracie

currently an inspiring teacher of nature connection
(and her grandchildren's grandchildren).

CONTENTS

FOREWORD

"I don't need to go to church. I worship God far better in the forest." As a minister living in Flagstaff, Arizona—a mountain community built around outdoor activities—I hear this refrain constantly. Despite my vocation, the sentiment resonates with me. At the same time, I don't believe nature unassisted can provide all the elements of a healthy, well-balanced spiritual life. Solitary rambles don't offer me the chance to be a part of a community, to connect with other worshipers; ritual is another worship element I don't find when I'm alone in the woods. Still, I often commune most deeply with God when I'm in a natural setting—and yet I continue to believe in the value of corporate worship. *Forest Church* offers me a bridge between these two aspects of my spirituality.

But it goes a step further. I've collected a plethora of books that attempt to answer the question, "How can faith communities succeed in the twenty-first century?" Most of these books fail to jump the theory-to-practice gap. Followers of Jesus seem to be sailing into a whirlpool of postmodern culture with no navigation plan. In the midst of this dilemma, Forest Church is truly a Godsend. It offers us a new way to think about our faith as Christ-followers, a way that includes both the worship of God in nature and the blessings of community and ritual. For people of faith who have lost touch with the Earth, *Forest Church* gives practical ways to reconnect, while eco-minded folks who have lost touch with the Divine within nature will find new perspectives to perceive God's glory. For the vast number of people fed up with "institutional religion," the

Forest Church movement promises an organic structure freed from professional clergy, dogmas, and formality. Wherever we are on these spectrums, *Forest Church* gives us practical, simple suggestions for exploring both nature and faith in new ways.

Forest Church has the potential to bring about both cultural change and personal transformation. Wilderness worship experiences may not be for you—but this will still be a hard book to put down once you begin reading. Bruce Stanley has thought deeply about the ways that humans and God connect in natural settings, and his synthesis of science, sociology, and spirituality is wide and intelligent, extending from the post-Ice Age agricultural transformation to ecological philosophy, from Druid rituals to the Bible. He also has deep spiritual insights, offering an easy-to-understand roadmap to a modern "nature mysticism," a twenty-first-century version of the spirituality of mystics such as Francis of Assisi and Nicholas of Cusa, one that harmonizes easily with ancient Celtic and Native American spiritual ways. He shares his understandings with clarity and conviction, presenting them as nonjudgmental invitations to go deeper, rather than a list of new obligations that might merely constrict our lives further.

Forest Church invites us to open not only our hearts and minds to God's voice but also our senses. It reminds us to pay attention to wind and birds as they perform their symphonies of praise. It nudges us down a path we may have abandoned when we became adults, one that's filled with wonder and joy. It tells us we can become children again, playing in the natural world—and that we will find Divine love waiting for us there, revealed in sky and earth, leaf and stream.

—**Kenneth McIntosh**, author of *Water from an Ancient Well: Celtic Spirituality for Modern Life* and leader of the new Flagstaff Forest Church

INTRODUCTION

The ideas explored in this book came into focus for me during a conversation with Paul Cudby (of Ancient Arden Forest Church) in April 2012. We'd both been thinking along similar lines under the heading "Forest Church." Since then a lot has happened, not least the formation of a growing number of Forest Church branches around the UK and beyond, of different flavors and styles.

My own focus is on nature connection as a foundation, with an underlying ethic toward living lightly—but there are other legitimate expressions of Forest Church which I have explored. This book is written for someone motivated to do something similar, but you can select your own level of involvement. Some people want to make a career out of Forest Church, while some people will just want to lead an afternoon of activities during a youth camp. The book is suitable for both.

In writing the book, I've had the following people particularly in mind:

- Facilitators and participants of Forest Church groups.
- Individuals wanting to connect with God in nature.
- Existing churches exploring a different style of service.
- Retreat centers and leaders wanting to offer something different.
- Youth workers looking for new ideas and activities.

- Friends or family groups looking to connect more with nature, during the year or while on vacation.
- People leaving an existing religious practice who feel it isn't in touch with nature or environmental issues.
- People outside the organized church who are looking for a nature-based group practice in the Christ tradition.
- Those from Druid, Pagan, or Earth Spirituality paths who would like to see another perspective or explore opportunities for deeper communication and understanding with Christians.

WHAT IS FOREST CHURCH?

A simple definition might be a group of people, outside, connecting with nature and worshiping God—but I don't think that quite captures the magic, so a bit more detail is needed.

Forest Church isn't just normal church happening outside; instead it attempts to participate with creation. We aim to learn, worship, meditate, pray, and practice with the trees, beside the creek, along the shore. Participants come with an attitude of experimentation, playfulness, and readiness to connect with nature. God is present in creation and can be understood through creation; you're *in* the sermon, the readings come from the Second Book of God. The worship will happen when your heart is caught up in the beauty of the moment.

Forest Church is a fresh expression of church, drawing on much older traditions when sacred places and practices were outside—but it is also drawing on contemporary research that highlights the benefits of spending time in wild places.

A few distinct versions of Forest Church are already emerging. Some people are taking a structured and liturgical approach to their events; others are simply providing a space with very little structure. Some people are facilitating groups who are strong on meditative or ritualistic practice; others have more of a field ecology focus on the flora and fauna around them. Some people are offering something distinctly Christian, while some are closer to the fringes. Some groups meet for an hour and a half, and some meet all day.

Location shapes each group as well. Some groups have to take into consideration the dangers of their local environment and the creatures living there. The setting might be rural or urban. Forest Church isn't bound by location; it's as possible in the city as in the middle of nowhere. *And no, you don't need a forest.*

Having said all that, I would argue that there are, or should be, some central ideas underpinning a generic understanding and description of Forest Church.

Puts safety first. Forest Church should always be safe, both for participants and for nature. Think about any potential hazards in the environment. Consider the impact your visit will have on the environment you are visiting.

Happens outside, in nature. In challenging weather, with a new group, most folks will be tempted to move inside if they have that option. Instead, if you plan ahead and get the clothing, setting, and activity right, weather won't matter so much.

Participates with nature. The aim isn't to *go into* nature as if it is something separate from us. Instead, the idea is to let the barriers drop; to *be with* nature. This is explored more in chapter 3.

Creates worship events that are site specific. Gatherings should relate and be in dialogue with the specific setting where they occur. If what is happening could have just as easily happened inside, it might be wonderful—but it isn't really Forest Church.

Allows time for nature to contribute. Nature cannot be scheduled; it speaks when *it* wants to. Build flexibility into events to allow this interaction to happen. This will develop as your group does. Adult often have to relearn the ability to listen, while children do it naturally. In many ways, children can be our teachers as we explore our connection with nature.

Recognizes that God is revealed in nature. *Since the creation of the world, God's invisible qualities—God's eternal power and divine nature—have been clearly seen, being understood from what has been made* (from Romans 1). The idea is that we can explore the characteristics of the Creator by exploring the creation.

Also recognizes that God *speaks* through nature. Nature is a form of living scripture. We may need discernment and practice to hear and interpret meaning, but nature is a source of Divine revelation (more on this in chapter 2).

Aims to be regenerative in practice. Forest Church should try to mend some of the damage humankind has done to the natural world without making things worse. Picking up more litter than we drop is a simple example, as is offsetting any carbon spent by the Forest Church event.

Exists within the Christ Tradition. Your wording might be different from mine, but the intention of those operating under the Forest Church banner (via www.forestchurch. co.uk) is for Forest Church to have a Christ-centered vision at its core.

There are various expressions of Forest Church, from occasional events hosted by an existing church, to groups that operate independently. These independent groups may need to explore the question, "Is it church?" The answer all depends on how you define "'church," but there isn't anything that a traditional church can do—such as worship, fellowship, teaching, prayer, discipleship and the sacraments (communion and baptism for example)—that can't be done by Forest Church. (Exactly *how* to do all that isn't covered in this book, however.)

The potential for Forest Churches is exciting. They cost nothing to set up; they're fairly easy to start; and they're potentially free to run. They often attract a diverse group of participants, some of whom wouldn't attend a traditional church.

PARTICIPATING

If you're a long way from any Forest Church groups, you may find that others near you would be interested in helping you start one. Also, Forest Church doesn't have a monopoly on group expressions of spirituality with strong ties to nature; you may want to consider other options instead. Five examples worth exploring are pilgrimages, various forms of Celtic spirituality, retreats in natural settings, Christian walking and other outdoor activities, and Christian ecology or conservation groups.

This edition of the book focuses on North American settings, with the hope that others from different parts of the world will find it useful. (A UK version of the book is also available.) I apologize for any frustration a southern hemisphere reader might have over the different timings for the seasons within the year.

The book doesn't contain footnotes, but there are in-line references to source material where relevant, and at at the end of the book are links, organized by subject, to further resources.

I've used the word "I" and "we" in this book, and when I'm addressing the reader directly, I say "you." This doesn't mean that "I" know better than "you," or that I'm sure "we" share the same ideas. I'm just using a conversational tone!

I'm not a churchman. (In fact, I'm positively unchurched.) Neither am I a knowledgeable naturalist or experienced environmentalist (nor much of a scholar). What I am is an enthusiastic seeker for a spiritual practice that engages authentically with people in today's environmentally challenged world. I am passionate about creating a practice that allows humans to connect with the magic of the created natural world infused with Divine presence. As John Muir put it,

I'd rather be in the mountains thinking about God,
than in church thinking about the mountains.

Thanks to my early readers, to my Mid Wales and Green-belt test subjects. And thank *you* for reading—see you among the trees some time.

Bruce Stanley
December 2012
Llangurig, Cambrian Mountains, Wales, UK

Chapter 1
Why Go Outside?

Earth's crammed with heaven,

And every common bush afire with God;

But only he who sees, takes off his shoes.

Elizabeth Barrett Browning

If you asked me to describe a transcendent moment, the first one that jumps to mind is always the tree of jewels that stopped me in my tracks one spring morning. If I thought about it harder I might have remembered a more iconic example from a retreat on Iona, a sunset in Cornwall, or my first experience of the Alps, but the tree is always first in my mind.

I saw it during a crisp, very still, early-spring mountain bike ride through the Forest of Dean. The undulating route we were on turned a corner and began to descend. There in front of me was a young birch lifting up its smoky, purple sprays, each bud, each twig holding a perfect drop of water, each water drop holding a miniature panorama and the bright morning sun. I stopped for a moment, I don't know how long, while I was utterly absorbed into a sense of connection with the Spirit who was both in this intimate magical moment and timelessly behind the whole Universe.

For some years I've been asking other people about their most perfect, transcendent moments; I ask them to tell me about the *thin places* they've experienced, those places where the boundaries between heaven and earth are at their most transparent. I find that most people's descriptions of these moments and places always are connected with nature. (I've yet to hear many descriptions of these moments occurring during religious services in buildings.) Usually, these moments don't last long, and they often seem to happen when the person is involved in something out of the ordinary; perhaps she's somewhere she's not been before or she's involved in an absorbing activity. What interests me most about these transcendent moments is that they are almost universal; nearly everyone I speak with has had some sort of experience like this. These "thin places" provide a common ground for shared experience of what some people call the revelation of God in creation (although it is also possible to have these experiences and attribute no Divine significance to them).

Nature is a doorway into the other-than-human world, a place inhabited by more than plants and animals. The natural world reveals secrets about its Creator, and God speaks to us through the wild and untamed world. Nature is sacred space.

Evidence in the European landscape indicates that earlier societies understood this. Towns built around sacred natural features are common. Bronze and Iron Age sites cluster around features in the natural landscape; sacred trees, some thousands of years old, still grow next to holy places. In North America, First Nations people still recognize the holiness of mountains, the spiritual significance of water and wood, rock and river.

But for most of us who live in the modern Western world, worship and ritual have become synonymous with the inside spaces of temples and churches. By enclosing our spiritual practices, we have separated ourselves from one of the greatest, most vibrant sources of Divine revelation.

How did that happen? The answer may be in your fridge.

THE FOOD STORY AND THE SACRED LAND

The story of our relationship with sacred landscape, nature, and place is intimately linked to the story of our food. A few generations ago, this statement would have seemed quite obvious. The evidence was all around; even our measurement system was originally based on the length of a stick used to steer oxen when ploughing the fields. But today we live in a different world. For the first time in human history, we're almost completely detached from the food story. We have little understanding of how food is produced or how it journeys from the fields to our plates. Our connection to the Earth is no longer obvious to us.

Until a few thousand years ago, humans were foragers, finely evolved hunter-gatherers. Farming started in the Middle East about ten thousand years ago, and over the next five or six thousand years the majority of the human population of the world became *food producers* rather than *food gatherers.*

Most people assume this was a step forward for humanity, that *food production* was more efficient and provided a surplus that freed people to do other things. This is surprisingly inaccurate. Archeological and anthropological research quoted in Colin Tudge's book *So Shall We Reap* indicates that skilled *food gatherers,* who knew their patch well, took far less time than *food producers* to gather the calories they needed. *The Earth And Its Peoples,* by Richard Bulliet of Columbia University, echoes these findings.

What about health and hunger? Surely the producers had it better than the foragers? The fossil record doesn't indicate that this is the case; instead, it actually shows a drop in the average height and age of death; the first food producers were four inches shorter and died seven years younger than their forager ancestors. (Figures given by Toby Hemenway, in a lecture given at Duke University in 2010.) What about the area required: isn't food production a more efficient use of the land? No, farming actually requires two to three times as much land as foraging.

In fact, the early food producers had it tough. Their diet decreased from a diverse range of nutritious foods to only a handful of foods. Agriculture meant settling in one place, which introduced disease through polluted water and domesticated animals. Soon after any area was converted to agriculture, the fertility of the soil would diminish, necessitating expansion. Farming families needed to be large to provide a workforce, and grain-based diets (porridge) meant babies could be weaned younger, allowing the next set of pregnancies to come along faster. Research by Theya Molleson at London's Natural History Museum shows that grain processing meant early arthritis and skeletal deformity for those at the grinding quern all day, while poor flour contaminated with sand wore down teeth. Some sources argue that agriculture even led to violence: it necessitated the police state to protect harvests, and motivated the expansion of empires in search of new fertile soils.

The food gatherers hadn't experienced famine with anything close to the same severity as the food producers now did. A good forager rarely goes hungry; there is always something to find, while the feedback from the system, if you're over-harvesting, is very quick. Conversely, terrible famine is still a part of the agricultural system where feedback is slower. Hemenway, in his lecture, explained that there were seven famines in the fifteenth century across Europe that reduced the population by 10 to 30 percent; the sixteenth century had thirteen of these famines, the seventeenth had eleven, and the eighteenth century had sixteen.

Clearly, the question isn't whether food production is better—it is: *Why did we ever make the change in the first place?*

Climate upheaval at the end of the last ice age was likely the cause of the change. Temperatures warmed so much that geologists gave the era since 9,000 BCE its own name: the Holocene. This change in the climate affected hunter-gatherers in some parts of the world less; Australia and North America, for example, maintained their food-gathering cultures.

But for most of Europe, the change was enormous. If you had been a *food gatherer,* you would have been relatively healthy, you would have worked less than half a week to harvest the food you needed, and you would have eaten from a broad range of foodstuffs. You would have been unlikely to experience famine. Your tribe would have been more culturally diverse, your family would have been smaller, and you would have been intimately connected with the natural world. As an early food producer, however, you would have worked much longer for your food. You would have been susceptible to an expanding range of new diseases. You would have been part of a big family, and if you were a woman, you would have had more babies. You would have spent a lot of your time in menial, repetitive activities, while your entire harvest was vulnerable to pests, drought, and disease. Life became a constant struggle against nature. You needed to know how to tame and dominate the natural world rather than work with it.

As a result of these changes in lifestyle, how would your understanding of God have changed? As human beings, our lifestyle and our relationship with food shapes the attributes we project onto God. For the foragers, God was in nature, the same nature in which they too participated. They lived in intimate harmony with the world around them, and so the spiritual hierarchy they envisioned didn't need to be very lofty. For the farmers and herders, however, God wasn't in nature anymore, and neither were they. Nature had become the enemy, something they hoped God would control—and as a result, they needed a more powerful God.

For the food producers, who had a harder time filling their bellies, God became important in a new way. Some seasons they were blessed, some seasons they faced hunger and even famine—and God was behind it all. Perhaps they were being punished for wrongdoing, they reasoned. Perhaps God wanted to be appeased.

Settling down on one geographical spot also affected humans' perception of sacred places. For the food gatherers, God would have moved with them as they traveled. The wild forests and waters, with their abundant offerings of sustenance, would have been viewed as holy places. As agriculture took over Europe, however, sacred places moved out of the forests to managed clearings. Eventually, via the barrows and later the stone henges (which might have had as much to do with commerce), our holy places moved indoors. Now we worshiped within the stone forests of cathedrals (whose architecture still echoed the arching trees and ethereal sky from which we had started).

Humans began to *make* sacred places rather than simply visit them. This was the beginning of the enclosing of spiritual practice. (Weather would have played a contributing factor as well. I facilitate a Forest Church in Mid Wales—an area known for its ability to rain for fifteen minutes every quarter of an hour!—and so I can well imagine the appeal of indoor worship.)

When we look back at the ancient practices of Western Europe, those of the "Pagan" or Celtic Bronze and Iron Age, some folks like to argue that we're seeing an authentic, original, indigenous, more harmonious belief system that Christianity wiped out. Historically, I don't think that's the case. The practices of the pre-Christian Pagans were part of a belief system created by food producers, people whose lives were still at odds with nature in the ways I've just described. Their spiritual beliefs and practices were developed to control nature in order to ensure the harvest. Historically, I don't think we can blame Christianity for turning us all into Earth-dominators. The change in the way humans live their lives is far more ancient.

The Industrial Revolution, with all its amazing inventions, its labor-saving machines and globe-spanning transportation, pushed us even farther away from our spiritual connections to the natural world. Today, we're living in strange times: unlike earlier generations of humans, we have been released from any direct connection with our own food production system.

As a result, our spirituality has been untethered from the stuff of life, from physical survival and the outdoors. Instead, it has become a practice of the emotion and intellect that's carried out indoors. Most people's accidental, informal transcendent moments—like mine on that early-spring bike ride—are out in the wild and beautiful world, and yet our intentional, formal spiritual practice happens both inside buildings and inside our heads, a double-glazed separation from the untamed green creation.

On Earth AS WELL AS in Heaven

Spirituality has, for some folk, become synonymous with a disembodied, introspective state of thoughts (or *no* thoughts), a separation of ego and awareness, as if God can be heard only when all sensory distractions are muted. The sensing, physical body, the natural part of us, is either a vehicle for carrying around our heads, where the real business of spirituality happens—or it's that annoying, hard-to-control bit attached to us that results in problems that the interior spiritual practice must overcome. Alternatively, the body is seen as merely a container for something far more important (energy, light, spirit), a perspective that rather denigrates the body.

All these divisions between body and spirit seem artificial to me. I don't believe this is the way we are meant to see ourselves and our place in the spiritual world. Spirituality becomes far more balanced when our entire being—head, heart, soul, and the sensing body—is involved *with* the world around us. "*Taste* and *see* that the Lord is good," scripture tells us; don't merely "*meditate*." Spiritual practices shouldn't be so celestial and airy that you lack a foundation and topple over, nor so material and temporal that you don't actually connect with God at all. Both perspectives are needed, and both can be unified in the way we connect to God and the world around us.

The tree of jewels that stopped me in my tracks on that bike ride highlights a gradual change in my own spirituality, from an interior practice dominated by mindfulness and contemplative prayer to a yearning for a more earthed and grounded practice with a greater physical connection to the world around me. I don't think I'm alone. More earthed spiritualities, such as Druidry and Paganism, are growing fast.

In December 2009, BBC Radio 4 ran a story recognizing that more people had taken part in the Winter Solstice celebrations than in the past millennium, with followers around the one hundred thousand mark. In 2010, the UK Charity Commission officially recognized Druidry as a religion, and in 2012, elements from a British Druid Order ritual were used in the closing ceremony of the Paralympics (and very good they were too).

One thing seems clear: there is a hunger and desire for a communal spiritual practice that connects with the earth and with a more manifest and creative God than the patriarchal, distant figure often presented by established Western religion—a God of the forest rather than a faraway heaven. We want the Friend who walked with us in Eden.

Pagan spiritual practices offer some people an answer to these yearning. If someone wants a practice within the Jesus Tradition that answers some of these desires, that explores what it means to participate *with* nature, then Forest Church is one such avenue. Why let the Pagans have all the fun?

Ecomindedness and Biophilia

A related, contemporary issue for many people is the search for a spiritual path that embraces today's ecological challenges. Many people are frustrated that established Western religions, not to mention society in general, often don't seem to be taking the Earth's serious problems as seriously and urgently as they should be. Some prominent groups and individuals within Christian circles are tackling these issues—but for the most part, the best we've come up with are rather limited behavioral change campaigns encouraging people to install new light bulbs. The problem with such campaigns for many people (myself included) is that our behaviors take their cues from our deeper beliefs and ways of being. As a result, we may adopt a change for a while, but sooner or later we revert to our previous default position. For some years now, reports on climate change from policy makers and international organizations have been calling for a "spiritual" change rather than a behavioral one. You'd imagine—wouldn't you?—in this secular age that most religions would jump at such invitations. . . .

Forest Church encourages people to participate with nature so that a shift may occur at a much deeper level—a spiritual change. What you love, you will care about. This may be naive, since our love is often imperfect, but it is at the very least a start, especially if we're open to the prompting of God, whose love *is* perfect.

Climb the mountains and get their good tidings.
Nature's peace will flow into you as sunshine flows into trees.
The winds will blow their own freshness into you,
and the storms their energy,
while cares will drop away . . . like the leaves of Autumn.
John Muir

Nature Deficit Disorder

Forest Church is not all about spirit, though. There are benefits to spending time outside, for our bodies and minds, as well as our souls. Some of these findings may seem to have come from the university of common sense, and yet they're often ignored or overlooked.

Nature deficit disorder is a useful label coined by American journalist Richard Louv. It describes a range of concerns, including young people's decreasing access to nature and the impact this has on them and on the wider society. He also explores nature deficit disorder within a range of adult issues such as mental health, convalescing, the creative process, and well-being.

Not surprisingly, nature deficit disorder can be countered by contact with nature. For some folks, that might mean time spent in wilderness areas, away from their ordinary lives. For others, the remedy might be as simple as stepping into the back garden or having lunch in a park. The not-insignificant benefits kick in within the first minutes of the nature connection.

Working against this are the habits, pressures, and busyness of the human world, which can easily dominate our good intentions to spend time in nature more regularly.

I've noticed that dog owners and people who grow their own food have an added incentive to actually get outside more often.

Another common problem we encounter when we do venture into the outdoor world is that we don't connect with nature because we're still in our heads, or we're busy traveling somewhere, or we're only interacting with the other humans with us. One of the most effective nature connection activities you can do is visit a daily "Sit Spot," a practice that couldn't be more simple. This and other nature connection activities are described in chapter 4.

Why does exposure to nature do us a world of good? The answers have been explored in other books at far deeper levels than what I'll offer here. The short answer is: we need to connect with nature because we are made that way. We lived in nature for the vast majority of our existence as a species; we are designed for the natural environment.

Some scientific research is exploring just how the nature connection is so nutritive. Evidence shows, for example, that hospital rooms with window views looking out on natural settings shorten hospital stays, and patients with access to nature have better pain control. Exposure to natural environments enhances our ability to cope with stress, illness, and injury. Research also indicates that exposure to natural places has antioxidant benefits; the longest-living people live very close to nature and its rhythms. (For more details, I recommend Richard Louv's book, *The Nature Principle.*)

Directed-attention fatigue is a term researchers use for a condition you get into when you're over-concentrating or focusing. It leads to irritability, compulsiveness, impatience, and making bad decisions (all of which just about describes me on a Friday afternoon after a long week of work). The antidote is time outside in the natural world. Recovery from mental fatigue and restoration of attention happens easily in nature. We have effortless attention in green spaces; the mind becomes balanced. Our senses all share in our perception of the world, which, incidentally, is also the optimum state for learning.

I recognized this most powerfully in my own life when I built my first polytunnel, a hoop greenhouse made from polyethylene plastic. For many years before this experience, I had been exploring mindfulness and contemplative practices to quieten my mind and connect with God—for example, by meditating on a kneeling stool for twenty minutes a day. During these moments, I was at least able to observe my own thoughts and their state of turbulence. Now, as the grow-your-own bug took hold at our home (which at that time was in a city) and we built our own little greenhouse in the garden, I discovered a new dimension to meditation that I had not yet experienced. The small space within the polytunnel, I found, was a delightful environment to visit, especially in the midst of the stressful focus of a workday. When the sun was shining, walking into the polytunnel was like stepping closer to the Equator; then, after a few months, this warm, fertile space was brimming with beans and tomatoes, with an understory of herbs and squashes. I realized then that after all the time it had taken me to develop an effective medita-tion practice, I had now found it here, effortlessly, just by stepping through the door into the polytunnel. Each time I entered, within seconds all my senses were activated. I wasn't consciously attempting to calm my thoughts, I was simply letting my attention rest on the next delight: a flower begin-ning to bloom, a tray of seedlings sprouting, the smell of basil, or the taste of an early strawberry.

Nature reverses and soothes directed-attention fatigue. You don't need a polytunnel or even a garden to achieve something similar—just the willingness to connect with the natural green spaces around you. How you make the connec-tion can differ from person to person and from time to time; deciding to make the connection is what matters. An area of interest or study can help (more about this in chapter 2). For me, that area of interest is most often foraging. For example, recently, while waiting outside a fairly uninspiring regional train station for a friend, I passed the time spotting the edible plants growing in forgotten little corners of the parking lot. This exercise refreshed my mind and occupied my thoughts. For someone else, it could be bird watching or cloud spotting or drawing. All these are good examples of flow activities.

FLOW

The kind of activities we do in nature—such as walking, cycling, drawing, running, climbing, foraging, tracking, playing, sailing, gardening, fishing, or navigating—are all flow activities. "Flow" is a well-developed concept from the work of psychologist Mihaly Csikszentmihalyi. Flow activities are good for your well-being.

The simple description of a flow activity is one where your skill level for the activity is in balance with the level of challenge the activity offers. If your skill level is too high and the challenge too low, the activity might result in boredom. If it is the other way around and your skill is too low for a high challenge, the activity might result in anxiety. If the two are well balanced, with the challenge nudging you along, the result is flow. As your skill increases, *flow* becomes *control*; if the challenge increases, *flow* becomes *arousal*. Control and arousal are good as well, but flow is the sweet spot.

Flow states are characterized by the challenge of the task suiting our skill level. We need to concentrate to do them. There are clear goals. We get immediate feedback. We have deep effortless involvement, and we feel a sense of control. In states of flow, our sense of self seems to vanish and time stops. These aspects are as true for mountain biking as they are for painting watercolors.

Unlike merely pleasurable activities—such as eating something tasty, receiving a massage, or looking at a beautiful view—we're actually changed and benefited by flow states. They help us store up cognitive resilience and mental well-being, like a charged battery that provides energy for another time. They also help us develop focus and concentration. For teenagers especially, flow states help develop mental control over the chaotic and often negative emotions common in adolescence. Young people encouraged to participate in flow activities are better able to concentrate and direct their attention when they become adults.

Flow isn't synonymous with outside activities. Flow can easily happen inside; reading, chess, indoor sports, cooking, and knitting could all be flow activities. But many flow states—such as those Forest Churches might encourage—do happen in the great outdoors.

These psychological benefits may not be the reason for engaging in Forest Church, but they are worth knowing about. They provide a foundation for why Forest Church and nature connections should happen, and they are the driving motivations for many people who want to participate.

And there's more to say about this. . . .

Brain Waves

Thinking takes place in four ways, resulting from four groups of brain waves, from fast and shallow, to slow and deep.

Fast and shallow *beta* brain waves are characteristic of the mind going about everyday things. Beta waves are an alert, waking state of consciousness. You'll be using them to read this book.

Alpha brain waves are next. They're created by the brain at particular moments, typically during relaxation. Taking a bath, daydreaming, and certain repetitive activities could all produce alpha waves. These brain waves are crucially important to the process of creativity and insight. (I'll come back to that later.)

Next are *theta* brain waves, the repository of unconscious thoughts, long-term memory, and emotion. You have these waves present all the time, including during dreaming sleep (unlike beta waves, which switch off during dreams). When you're experiencing theta waves, you'll find hidden creativity and the answers to problems—but you may also stumble over suppressed baggage and other issues. Theta waves are the mental activity that helps you find deep spiritual connection, insight, and the capacity for growth and healing.

The critical combination is when these three kinds of brain waves are present at the same time. Beta, the mental state where you can do something consciously with your ideas, is often present above theta, but you will need alpha waves to bridge the gap. Two of the times alpha brain waves are present are just as you drift off and when you wake up from sleep. As they fade away, so do your memories of dreams that your beta brain waves are hearing from your theta waves.

What's this got to do with nature? Alpha brain waves also occur in spaced-out moments during the day, such as those that characterize people's descriptions of transcendent moments, but more important, they occur during repetitive activities such as walking. That's the secret known to many scientists and composers: set the problem aside and go for a walk—and the answer seems to come. As the Greek philosopher Diogenes of Sinope said, "It is solved by walking." Many nature-connection activities, like walking, allow alpha brain waves to arise, leading to insights of creativity and spiritual depth.

The fourth level of mental activity, and the slowest, consists of *delta* waves. These are the unconscious mind, and they're common in people who have deep intuition and empathy—and also in people who seem to have what some would describe as a sixth sense. Sometimes they can offer us a deep unconscious awareness of danger. Children who grow up in abusive and unpredictable settings may develop strong delta waves. Delta insights are more expansive and connecting, reaching outside of ourselves more than theta waves do. They are important for a connection and participation beyond ourselves—with nature, for example.

Games, as well as ritualistic practices, can be useful for exploring these levels of consciousness and connection. Two games, called Body Radar and Silent Stalker, found in chapter 6, are particularly relevant.

WHATEVER YOUR REASONS

Those who are drawn to Forest Church practices will all have their own reasons and motivations. Some of us may be attracted by the positive benefits I've listed in this chapter. Others may be driven by the desire to escape from an existing model of doing church that has become uninspiring. These folk may not know what they're looking for so much as they know that the "normal" church experience no longer works for them.

It doesn't really matter whether you're motivated by wanting to learn more about local plants and animals . . . deepen your creativity . . . or simply sit on top a hill on midsummer's eve and drum with a group of like-minded friends. Whatever your motivation, God will meet you there.

CHAPTER 2

READING THE SECOND
BOOK OF GOD

The world around us is a mighty volume

wherewith God hath declared himself.

John Wesley

Nature is sometimes described as the Second Book of God. Some theologians (Augustine for example) may argue that it's the *first* book of God. Whichever way, while I do recognize the importance and authority of the sacred scriptures, I don't think they're the only revelation about God, and I don't think Jesus thought so either.

Before we talk about reading this Second Book, we need to understand what we mean when we use the word "nature." What *is* nature? You no doubt have an idea already, but your idea might not be the same as mine.

During a hike in my teens, I and two other lads were crossing a high, broad valley somewhere in the hills of South Wales. I remember stopping at one point, struck by the realization that in any direction, for a full 360 degrees, for the first time in my life I couldn't see anything human made. No buildings, no power lines, no fences. I remember finding this deeply significant, a wild place comprised wholly of nature. At the time, I didn't realize that of course the land showed many signs of human interference, the lack of trees being the most obvious, but you get my point.

For me, nature is being among the other-than-human world. I'm most drawn to mountainous areas, away from other people, and to the coast. At the coast, I might be walking across rocks or sand with no view of anything living, but it's still nature. At other times, nature might be a view from a window in the middle of a city where I can see a tree or a park. For some people, however, nature is viewed through a microscope or telescope, or it counts only if it's wild, virgin wilderness—hard to find these days. For the purposes of this book, whatever you first thought of will do as long as you realize that others may have another idea.

THREE WAYS IN

The following diagram shows three broad ways into reading nature, or of understanding God in and through nature.

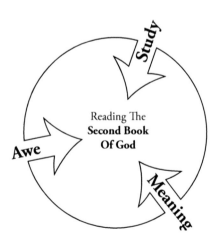

These ways aren't meant to indicate a linear process, with a start and end point; instead, each of these is a way to begin, and they all interrelate.

Moments of *Awe* are perhaps the least formal encounters with the Divine in nature but also the most powerful and absorbing. Many people have had such a moment. These moments seem to happen when people are participating in flow activities, or in moments of relaxation or daydreaming, when alpha brain waves are likely to be present. They commonly happen when people are on their own or not focusing on other people around them. Moments like these are not altogether accidental or unpredictable, since many natural places or phenomena seem to increase their chance of occurring. And it is undeniably the case that these moments seem to happen more often to people who meditate.

If *Awe* is characterized by the dumbstruck question, "Isn't it amazing?", then *Study* is characterized by the journalist's questions of "What, how, and why?" *Study* provides a more practical and cerebral way into nature connection. To be authentic, the area of Study has to be one we're intrinsically motivated to explore, one that delights us. Areas of Study are diverse, from common ones such as birds, plants, and horticulture, to more unusual ones such as foraging, natural navigation, and weather lore. As knowledge of your area of interest deepens, so does your capacity to find meaning in it and to experience Awe from it.

Meaning is about searching for insight and relevance: "What does it mean?" It is the most challenging of the three areas, as it requires both discernment and creativity. Very practically, it is the area in which we ask ourselves what God might be telling us through an element of the natural world, or what it might be telling us about God. Its challenges notwithstanding, Forest Church would be missing a vital element if we didn't explore what it all means. Meaning includes the subject of *natural theology,* learning about God, not through preexisting sacred texts but through knowledge and observation of the natural world, just as Jesus did from time to time.

When you put these three together practically and imagine moving from one to another, you will see between them other elements familiar in spiritual practice.

When captured by a transcendent, awe-inspiring moment, you might ask yourself what it means and explore its depths, which can lead to a heart full of worship. Study can deepen and speed up our reading of the world so that we're more often delighted and more often captured by Awe. Between Study and Meaning, moving between an analytical and a more philosophical mind, great leaps of creativity and insight can occur.

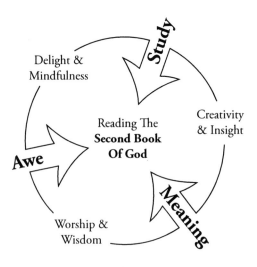

Reading nature is only one strand of nature connection. Most often it forms a foundation for other activities. Each of the three approaches is accessible to groups and individuals.

In this chapter we explore them as broad ways into reading the Second Book of God. Chapter 6 has some practical activities within each category suitable for groups, and chapter 4 has ideas more relevant for individuals.

AWE

Humans exist for awe's sake–to be radically amazed. . . .
There can be no living faith without it.

Matthew Fox

As I've suggested above, Awe—*transcendent* moments—can give us a deep and pervading sense of connection to something much greater than ourselves or our ordinary lives. They're difficult to put into words, but "wow" is often the word that comes to mind.

Transcendence can mean a number of things, from self-transcendence to an inaccessible transcendent realm. Transcendence, in our context, contains the idea that the barriers between heaven and earth, the lines between the physical and spiritual realms, have disappeared; the ordinary has become infused with something Divine; or our perception has changed, allowing us to see things differently.

Three distinctions are often used when speaking of transcendence. *Numinous* experiences relate to a connection or perception of something emerging, something wholly other or outside the physical, empirical world we know. *Mystical* experiences have their focus on the experiencing itself, a moment where perception has changed and great insights might occur, even though these might be difficult to put into words. *Epiphanic* experiences similarly describe a moment of privileged, out-of-this-world insight, but one that might relate to an area of study or questioning in which the person is already involved, a Divinely charged "aha!" moment.

The key questions for Forest Church are: How can you encourage these moments to happen? What should you do when you have one? What are they telling us about God? And what might God be telling us through them?

Practical answers to the first question (How can you encourage transcendent moments to happen?) are all to do with *approach* and *attitude*. There is a checklist of things *not* to take with you into nature if you're hoping to experience Awe. Leave behind your camera, phone, watch, agenda, mapped route, conversation, and your entire self (by which I mean the constant thinker you are most of the time). In other words, go mindfully, open and present to the reality around you. Allow your senses to be engaged and softly focused, holding a gentle alertness to the spirit of the place you're visiting. Our senses, rather than our mental activities (our thinking), are how we begin to overcome the separateness from nature we think we have. This is the first step to any deeper transcendent connection.

In my own experience, the frequency of these moments goes up the more I'm mindful and present, which points to the idea that a busy, anthropocentric, thinking mind is quite an effective barrier to having them.

When you find yourself experiencing a transcendent moment, don't talk, don't reach for a camera, don't turn to anyone else and try to get them to experience it too—just be present. These moments can occur anywhere, in a city, on a train or bus while looking out the window, on a mountain, in your garden—but some places become known specifically for them. The *sublime* and romantic movements in the nineteenth century had nature-based transcendent moments as their focus, taking people to beautiful locations to experience the Divine (for example, the Highlands of Scotland, the Lakes of Cumbria, and later the national parks of the United States).

These days you may find these locations marked on the map as tourist sites; they often have parking lots where visitors can get out to see the view. Typically, a car stops, someone gets out, and up comes the camera; the person imagine she's captured the moment to be enjoyed, presumably sometime later. Actually, however, she's lost any chance she had of experiencing a transcendent moment at all. A well-traveled TV producer once told me that the best holiday he ever had was one where he forgot to take his camera with him.

Approach and attitude are crucial, and for Forest Church, what these moments are saying about God, and what God might be saying to us, are also of real importance; as Abraham Heschel said, "*Awe is the beginning of wisdom.*" These questions sit under the *Meaning* heading later on, but as you move between the experience and its meaning, in that interplay other things occur, such as a deep sense of worship and prayer in the afterglow of the moment. I've never sung more loudly or meaningfully an old hymn or snippet of worship song than when I'm alone, on a hill, just after a moment of Awe.

STUDY

While we contemplate in all creatures,
as in a mirror, those immense riches
of his wisdom, justice, goodness, and power,
we should not merely run them over cursorily,
and, so to speak, with a fleeting glance,
but we should ponder them at length,
turn them over in our mind seriously and faithfully,
and recollect them repeatedly.
John Calvin

Study takes us from the experience that make us say "Isn't it amazing?" deeper into the question, "What is it?" Far from turning the nature connection into a head-based experience, Study actually seems to enhance Awe. Study can also be a starting point itself, leading to a new appreciation of nature.

Study areas fall into six categories. The first and most obvious is a *scientific* interest such as botany or geology, or a field-study focus like fungi or tracking. Similarly, it can be any of the off-the-shelf studies of birds or plants or animals. Or the Study category might be a *creative* focus you'd like to develop that would lead to a greater connection with nature. Drawing, photography, poetry, or even art and sculpture from found objects *in situ* are examples. The third Study category can be an *experiential* activity, such as climbing, sailing, woodcrafts or geocaching, that you want to develop, or it may be one that explores relevant *nature-sociological* studies such as ecology or permaculture. A development of the last category could be *nature-spiritual* studies of practices such as Druidry, Shamanism, Celtic Christianity, or First Nation beliefs. The sixth and final category for Study may be an *eco-therapy* such as ecopsychology or nature-based spiritual direction.

The question is: What is it that *you* would be delighted to learn more about? The question is deliberately aimed at you, the individual, since the deeper you go with a subject, the more it will become tailor-made to your own interests and passions, and the less it will be of relevance to other people. You might be lucky in finding other people in your group or circle of acquaintances who are equally interested; the danger, however, is that you risk boring the pants off other people if you don't recognize that your passion might not be theirs. Samuel Johnson had apparently had this experience when he quipped, "You teach your daughters the diameters of the planets and wonder when you are done that they do not delight in your company."

Introducing some of these Study areas to a Forest Church group, if done at an appropriate level and facilitated well, is of huge benefit, however. They are all ways into understanding nature and into reading the Second Book of God.

My long-standing passion, among many others, has been foraging. Practicing it has taught me a lot about God's provision and generosity, as well as lessons in trust, patience, and faith. As I first began to learn the uses of plants, being in nature was like being in a classroom, with all the trappings: lots of books and equipment to help identify plants. At this beginner's, head-based stage, mindfulness and the chance of any moments of Awe are slim. But once you internalize your learning and it becomes automatic, being present and mindful in nature is very much enhanced.

There are a few areas I would hope most people involved with Forest Church would study; they seem foundational to a basic understanding of nature. I'd include recognizing a basic list of plants, trees, birds, animals, and insects indigenous to your area, as well as possibly the geology of your region. I'd also include some knowledge and understanding of traditional countryside practices, since much of our land carries signs of the long history of human impact on it. Added to that are the festivals and beliefs associated with the seasons, both Pagan and Christian. I'd also encourage people to get involved with growing some of their food, either directly or through a local community growing scheme. The reasons for this can be surmised from the opening chapter of the book.

When you start exploring Study areas, there are some less well known ones that might tickle your fancy. Here are just six examples, but there are many more. You should be able to discover one that's right for you.

Bird language: This isn't about identifying particular species; it is about learning what the calls are communicating. Prey animals, such as a deer in woodland, learn to expand their awareness far beyond what they can see by listening to birds. The calls birds make range from companion calling— "everything is okay" messages—to various alarms. Experts in bird language can even tell you what sort of danger (hawk, snake, fox, etc.) the alarm call is signaling.

Natural navigation: Finding your way without maps, compass, or GPS. Nature has far more clues to direct you than you might think, including the movement of the sun and the stars, the way plants grow, the way spiders spin their webs, and the temperature of rocks.

Landscape reading: This is about seeing into the story that any given landscape is telling you, from its underlying geology, to the story of humans' use of the land. It includes reading the soil by the plants that are growing on it, as well as understanding the practices and beliefs that led to various landscape features (more on this in chapter 6).

Weather lore: From cloud spotting to predicting the weather for the next few days, weather lore has many interesting facets. Stronger outdoor smells, for example, might indicate low pressure, which could prompt you to remember that your own heightened body odor will act like a beacon to biting insects.

Land art: This creative Study area links the making of a piece of art with the landscape it's in. More often than not the art is made from found objects within the landscape. It can be as simple as a design from fallen leaves to sculptures made from slate that channels water. Some people compose music to go along with natural settings. Andy Goldsworthy, Richard Long, and David Nash are some of the more famous proponents of this kind of creativity, and they are also good sources of inspiration.

Permaculture: This environmentally friendly Study looks at how humans can interact with nature to produce what they need while caring for the earth. In many ways, such as the related practice of forest gardening, the idea is to mimic patterns and closed systems from nature for our own systems, from food production to whole community considerations such as transport, power, and waste.

One reason facilitators or nature-based spiritual directors need to know the basics (common plants, trees, habitats, processes and patterns, animal and bird characteristics, etc.) is to help other people explore Meaning, especially if they sense God is speaking to them but they can't figure out what is being said. If someone tells the facilitator that he saw a hawk being chased by some colorful birds the shape of crows through a wood with lots of acorns, a facilitator who has a knowledge base from Study will be able to help him unlock some of the Meaning hidden in that scene. Study is often the foundation for Meaning.

MEANING

Great are the works of the Lord; they are pondered by all who delight in them.
Psalm 111:2

Consider the lilies...
Jesus

In the context of reading the Second Book of God, *Meaning* is about discerning God's messages in and through nature, asking what the creation reveals about its Creator. This kind of communication happens in two ways: it is initiated by us or by God.

When *we* initiate the search for Meaning we can either use something from nature to illustrate an idea we are already exploring—like Jesus did when referring to wild flowers in Luke 12—or we can choose to explore the Meaning of something in nature from a position of neutral inquiry (if such a thing is possible). It may follow naturally from an area of Study, so that we begin to ask, "What is this telling me about God?" Neither of these two ways of exploring God seem to be much practiced in these anthropocentric, post-enlightenment days. I can't remember ever hearing a tree quoted or the meaning of a mountain used in a meditation or sermon.

When *God* initiates the communication, or sends us a message through nature, we need to be listening in the first place. We need to be, first of all, open to the idea that God might be able to speak to us. Second, we need to be in connection enough with nature to spot the message, not so preoccupied by the human world that we aren't receptive to anything from the other-than-human world. God-initiated communication might occur in a number of ways. It could be a bolt out of the blue, when something from nature captures our attention very definitely and our intuition tells us that God is saying something through it; the challenge, then, is to work out what it means. Second, we might be pondering a question or seeking some guidance . . . and we take that seeking into nature, open to the idea that God might speak to us somehow through nature. There are also less direct, more everyday messages not necessarily directed at us as individuals, through which God might be speaking more generally to humanity—rainbows, for example.

These ideas are going to face plenty of criticism. For example: finding the Divine in nature isn't scientific or quantifiable. It's too close to superstition, geomancy, or shamanistic fortune telling. It places too much weight on the interpreter's subjective understanding. When we connect with the

Divine through the Bible, the First Book of God, we have the benefit of centuries of academic study, libraries of commentaries and theology, advanced university courses, symposiums, journals—and the source material is written down. With the Second Book of God we can't rely on the traditions and writings of those who have gone before us; we have only some evidence that the early desert teachers, mystics, and Celtic saints practiced this way of relating to God. The source material is a fleeting phenomenon—or it has leaves and bark . . . or feathers . . . or fur . . . or it won't sit still.

Some resources—books and packs of cards found in the body-mind-and-spirit sections of bookstores—will tell you what the oak tree or coyote or deer means symbolically. I wouldn't dismiss these, as they are attempts to achieve what I'm encouraging, but neither would I treat them as any authority unless they've come from a very deeply nature-connected writer or tradition. A more helpful body of work, one step removed from direct natural source material, consists of the rituals and practices that have their inspiration in nature and its rhythms. Christian, Pagan, and country-side traditions can shed light on the Divine-nature-human Meaning-making practice.

But these are all secondary sources. The primary source is your direct contact with nature and its Creator.

The task of interpretation and Meaning-making places a challenge on the interpreter—but be encouraged: when we look at Jesus, seeing him as a theologian, rather than as the subject of theology—we find that he was very comfortable with these practices.

At the same time, of course, he was deeply rooted in scripture and its interpretation. I would recommend the same for any Forest Church participant, for the same God who speaks to us in nature has revealed much already in the Bible, and the two messages, if authentic, aren't going to contradict each other.

Still, Jesus did not rely *only* on scripture. His teaching demonstrates a real and deep *natural theology*, and he often made a point about God or the Kingdom not by quoting examples from preexisting texts but by drawing on the natural world around him to make and reveal meaning.

NATURAL THEOLOGY

The sun, the moon, the stars, the seas, the hills and the plains—
Are not these, O Soul, the Vision of Him who reigns?

Alfred, Lord Tennyson

Natural theology is nothing new. It was very popular in the Romantic movement, until the Enlightenment challenged it so robustly it seemed to fall apart. The Romantics had assumed that nature could self-evidently prove the existence of the Christian God, which didn't stand up to much scrutiny, especially when you got down to the nitty-gritty of the rather unchristian, brutal goings-on of one natural creature exploiting another.

Like the Romantics, you too may always have thought that nature proves the existence of God. You may be right, within the context of your life, but the basis for your "proof" is your own preexisting interpretive framework. I agree with Alister E. McGrath in his book *The Open Secret, A New Vision for Natural Theology*, that we need to accept that there is no such thing as an unbiased interpretive perspective. A Christian cosmology can hugely help in the search for Meaning as long as we know we're seeing through biased eyes. Knowing this should dissuade us from ever doing what I refer to as public *we*-ing: "*We* can see that this oak tree is telling *us* such-and-such about God." You might indeed be able to see it, but you risk antagonizing anyone else who doesn't see nature through the same perspective. People become understandably uncomfortable when someone else's perspective is jammed down their throats.

Participants of Forest Church find both an immediate, instinctive way into discerning Divine Meaning in nature and a deeper, more considered route. The latter involves *Study* that we've explored previously: the more you know about the characteristics, patterns, and habits of a subject, the more you may be able to discern its Meaning.

For example, the birch tree I mentioned at the beginning of this book was central to a moment of *Awe* for me. Later, when I began foraging, I *Studied* birch and its uses. Its character as a tree is of pioneering generosity. It is the first tree to colonize an area after the retreat of ice, and it lives for only a short period, reproducing fine seeds prolifically, until it dies, rotting quickly, producing an ecosystem for the process of succession. The farther north you go, the more the birch's uses are understood, from its sweet sap's many edible uses to it's root's detoxing tea. Its bark provides flour, paper, and waterproof shoes, beakers and boats. I've spent a lot of time with birch (we grow hundreds of them on our land), and I talk about them often when taking groups foraging. When I explore their *Meaning,* as part of a Forest Church tea ceremony, for example, many ideas always jump to my mind, but more often than not, for me, they simply represent God's blessing on our beginnings, God's generosity and lightness of touch. In more personal situations, I've often found birch to be present in fleeting, liminal moments when I'm aware of a simple reminder of God's love, almost as if the birch were a captured hint of the reality of the Spirit's presence.

The more immediate, instinctive, specific way to find Meaning is to be present with the inquiry. Without any studied knowledge about the aspect of nature involved in the exercise, simply, prayerfully, mindfully ask yourself what you think it means. Open yourself to the answer.

One summer, I'd come into the long barn where we live and left the door open behind me. A swallow followed me in, making two lightning-quick circuits of the space before leaving. It was a delightful hit-and-run display of acrobatic brilliance. My intuition told me that Meaning was to be found in this fleeting visitation, but I couldn't work out what. The following day, in a less busy moment, I stopped and asked the question, "What do I feel it means?"—and the sobering, Job 33-like answer came to me: for me, the swallow's swift flight was a message about my impermanence here, and therefore a call to humility. Furthermore, I realized that generations of those swallows will be around long after I've gone from this barn.

Reading signs from God in nature was fairly common practice among the Celtic saints. Contrary to the common idea that early Christians plonked their settlements on top of preexisting sacred sites, many were placed where the saint in question received a sign from God in nature. Ravens on a tree, a white sow in a clearing, crickets on a bramble plant, and a bear in the woods marked the locations of sites ranging from chapels to cities. And no doubt there were more prosaic examples that never made it into recorded history.

A quick note of caution here: when we attempt to read natural events such as earthquakes and other natural disasters as God's judgment on one group or another, we are often making an unhelpful projection of human prejudice in the guise of natural theology.

So how to begin to experience natural theology? Start off simply: ask God to give you eyes to see and ears to hear. In other words, be open to messages from nature and ask for Divine help when interpreting them.

When my wife Sara and I were looking for somewhere to live with a bit of land, we were seeking a sign that would point us in the right direction. After many months and many miles of looking, we found a place that seemed right—and we noticed four signs that confirmed for us that it was the right place. One was the sound of a stream, the second was a rabbit, the third was a flock of starlings, and the fourth was wild yarrow growing on the land—all carrying specific Meaning for us. These gave us confidence that this was the right place, and we made an immediate offer.

The challenge is interpretation. Study and knowledge of nature and its language help. Seeing nature with something of Christ's perspective helps. But in the end, it comes down to discernment and practice . . . and making space to notice nature in the first place. At the very least, make a practice of using something you've noticed in nature as a prompt for prayer or meditation. When reading the Second Book of God, why not borrow techniques used to read the First Book of God, such as Lectio Divina, a book-by-book study, or a meditation on a theme. Have fun applying these exercises to nature.

CHAPTER 3

PARTICIPATING WITH NATURE

O God, enlarge within us
the sense of fellowship with all living things,
even our brothers, the animals,
to whom Thou gavest the earth
as their home in common with us.
We remember with shame that in the past
we have exercised the high dominion of man
with ruthless cruelty so that the voice of the earth,
which should have gone up to thee in song,
has been a groan of pain.
May we realize that they live, not for us alone,
but for themselves and for Thee
and that they love the sweetness of life.
Basil the Great (329–379)

The highest heavens are the Lord's," says Psalm 115:16, "but the earth hath he given to the children of men." I'm not sure we're up to the responsibility.

A big shift in my thinking about the human and nature connection happened during a permaculture design course. Permaculture is a design strategy for human and nature systems (such as food production and environmentally friendly housing), from a domestic to a community-wide scale, with an ethical foundation expressed as *people care, earth care,* and *fair share.*

An idea central to permaculture is that value in nature should be recognized and protected. Taking something of high value, such as expensively purified water to flush the toilet, or electricity to keep appliances on standby, or a tree to become pulp, is wasteful when the energy used to purify water may have other effects on the environment, electricity uses up natural resources, and a tree could maintain its value and become a number of other things in its lifetime before it ends up as pulp. Primarily, permaculture is all about recognizing true value in the first place.

One of my permaculture teachers was Ben Law, of *Grand Designs* fame, with his self-built, round-timbered house. During my time with him, the biggest part of his teaching focused on the value of the twelve-acre sweet chestnut grove he manages. He held up a stick, roughly a foot long and as thick as his thumb, the sort of thing you'd throw on a bonfire when cleaning up your yard, and he used this stick to illustrate the value of natural resources we might otherwise consider waste. The winter before, he said, he had taken a basket of these sticks to a Christmas fair, with a price tag attached to each for a few pounds and a label saying, "English Boomerang—just add a dog."

But we can take a step beyond our human-centered, utilitarian views and recognize nature's intrinsic value, as something of worth in its own terms. The dominant view in the Western world is that growth, development, and value are measured financially, which is an anthropocentric view of nature merely as a resource to be managed for human interests. This, of course, is challenged by more ecocentric views that have been around for a long time, and I won't rehearse them here. What I would like to explore is how the ecocentric or participative position relates to Forest Church and an individual's experience of God in nature. It is of fundamental importance. The call to participate with nature encompasses Forest Church; it's not an option within it.

The aim of connecting with God through nature begins with connecting with nature itself—and the deepest expression of that is to connect as participant, to be *with* nature, rather than to go *into* nature as somehow separate from it. This can be very difficult to do, since much of our formation as adults, and the continuing influence and structure of society, is anthropocentric. A few people do seem to demonstrate with ease the participative approach; those people are mostly between one and five years old. I'm lucky enough to be living with one, and she is my most influential teacher of nature connection.

Why participate? Think of any practical or experiential element of your life, not just sports or driving a car or physical hobbies but also relationships: being a family member, dancing, going to a party. With each of these, it is through participating that you learn the most. Other ways of learning apply, but developing love and passion for something is particularly strong at the participatory level. Equally, to know yourself loved in return occurs deeply through this participatory interplay. The same applies to us and nature.

Participating with nature has an ethical and practical dimension. Much of what Forest Church does, particularly if you're a participant rather than a facilitator, falls into the practical dimension (chapters 4 and 6 are full of example activities). In this chapter, we'll explore the ethical dimension further. The emphasis here is on the ecocentric foundations of Forest Church and how participating might lead to a fairer, kinder relationship with nature in the rest of our lives.

From Dominator to Participant

A helpful way of exploring a fuller definition of the *participant* is to look at a few of the other possible positions along a continuum. The following four ethical positions are adapted from the work of Dutch philosopher Petran Kockelkoren.

I am a dominator of nature: I believe that nature is for supporting the existence of the human race. It is merely a source of raw materials to serve human goals and to be conquered, controlled, subdued, and domesticated. I seek the maximum utility and profit that is legally and economically possible.

I am a steward of nature: I see nature from a human perspective, but unlike the dominator, I recognize definite limits. I am entrusted with the use of nature, not with its consumption. I have a duty of care for organisms other than humans. I consider that human interests prevail over those of animals and plants, but the interests of plants and animals are more than just economic, so I set limits on my use. My duty of care extends to species conservation and protection of ecosystems to the extent that, sometimes, human interests must yield, to avoid putting nature out of joint.

I am a partner with nature: Animals are potential allies, so they have their own say. Nature is an interplay of life forms, in which each invests its own expressiveness and intrinsic value. I am separate from nature in that I am free to have a conscious relationship and ethical attitude toward it. The partnership isn't exactly balanced, because it consists of life forms interacting at different levels of complexity. I practice sustainable organic or ecological care for nature and use technology as long as animals aren't unnaturally forced.

I am a participant with nature: I exist within a mix of interdependent and interwoven life forms. I am an integral part of nature. I respect other organisms, not only because of their intrinsic value but because of nature's overall complexity. The countless relationships and balances among organisms have a value greater than their use to human beings. I am ecocentric when setting limits to my interventions in nature and attempt to be regenerative rather than merely sustainable. I intervene in nature for the purpose of food production, but when I do I try to work with the inherent dynamism of natural processes.

Where would you place, within these four positions, your average multinational food producer, oil company, environmental charity, local organic food producer, politician, and yourself? I've had very few people ever position themselves as participants in their wider lives, and neither could I. As I said before, it is an extremely challenging position to achieve, not least because the infrastructure of our society makes it so difficult.

But it is imperative that we have it as a goal. I've long since despaired of the prevalent use of the word "sustainable" as if it represents an acceptable aim. Instead, I'd argue for the word "regenerative"; we have a long way to go before we get back to something that can then be "sustained." Also, participation doesn't subordinate human needs; it expresses the possibility that both parties can get their needs met within the process.

Participants in Forest Church do not point fingers; they don't call attention to so-and-so's terribly un-eco behavior. Instead, we work to enable people to participate with nature, to fall in love with it. What you love, you may be better motivated to care about, even delighted to care about. This involves a attitudinal change; a reprogramming at a deeper level.

Humans are resistant to change. We see the merits, values, and arguments for doing something differently, such as creating a healthier or more environmentally friendly life-style. But when it comes to the crunch, change is difficult to initiate or sustain. Philosophers and psychologists have come up with many metaphors for this aspect of the human being, but my favorite is Jonathan Haidt's, from his book *The Happiness Hypothesis*. This change-resistant dynamic within us, says Haidt, is like a rider on an elephant. The rider is that future-thinking, values-driven, conscious, logi-cal part of us that weighs the arguments and recognizes the merits of a different way of being. But the rider seems igno-rant of the fact that she is sitting on an elephant: the auto-matic, ancient, habitual, present-moment, animalistic part of us. The rider makes lofty plans and goals, but unless the elephant changes its course, the rider gets nowhere. Eventu-ally, the elephant always gets its way—a few weeks after the grand resolutions of New Year, for example.

But there are some practical elephant-training tech-niques. The elephant is moldable—and if you've changed someone's elephant, the rider comes too. Mindfulness medi-tation and cognitive behavioral therapy are two examples of elephant reprogramming, but another seems to succeed by making the changes so gradual and small that the elephant doesn't recognize that it's happening.

These are regular, small, low-level, delight-driven, incre-mental steps, which are characteristic of participating in an activity, such as someone attending Forest Church. One exponent of this method is the Japanese management tech-nique called Kaizen which was instrumentally successful in the postwar period for turning around Japan's fortunes, not by forcing workers to drastically change, but by very gen-tly making very small improvements under the elephant's radar—all of which added up to a big change in the end.

Participation can enable effective change and elephant reprogramming. That with which we are participating—nature—is actually a process and a spiritually charged one at that. This, however, may be somewhat at odds with our default idea of nature.

PARTICIPATING IN NATURE AS PROCESS

Time-lapse photography is a popular technique in wild-life documentaries. By speeding up the action, it reveals the astonishing process of growth and movement made by plants climbing, opening, and seeking the light. We're taken by surprise by such definite aliveness because we don't normally notice it. Any movement we usually perceive in nature is caused by the wind or is so gradual it is discernible only on a seasonal scale. Otherwise, nature appears to be fairly static; even the animals that move about, as players on its stage, are somehow unchanging and predictable. Familiar countryside, like a favorite beautiful spot or park or picnic site, even national parkland, are held in a state of suspended succession. To our eyes, they look the same as they did ten years ago and as they will in ten years' time.

We like it that way. In fact, we work hard to keep it that way. When we see empty lots and derelict spaces that are left to succession, for one reason or another, they stand out like sore thumbs, as if they were the natural equivalent of crass vandalism. It's as if we sense the wild and uncontrolled is about to assert itself and take over (as we know deep down it eventually will), and we don't like to be reminded of it. Despite the work and resources involved, we keep the natural spaces closest to us in a perpetual state of an ecosystem's equivalent of infancy. We don't let them mature or change.

The time-lapse sequence seems to us like a trick, a disturbing alien view that makes us uncomfortable, as if it's contradicting our normal perception of the natural world as just a green, unchanging space. We're more comfortable with our never-changing, snapshot idea. No camera can record what's really going on, though; Spirit doesn't show up on film.

To participate with nature we must recognize that nature is a process of relationships, never static, always dynamic. The Second Book of God is alive; open it today and it reads differently from how it did yesterday. It's interacting with such complexity that we're hardly able to comprehend it, but it can be sensed. I've personally never found real magic in darkened rooms with archaic symbols, but I *have* found it in the forest or along the shore or in my back yard.

At the participatory level, consciousness itself may extend through heightened senses and in ways we don't easily understand, perhaps using delta brain waves as mentioned in chapter 1. There are astonishing stories from around the world of deeply nature-connected people; for example, the isolated Moken people of the Andaman Islands in the Indian Ocean, who knew long in advance that the 2004 tsunami was coming. Or the U.S. troops who had spent significantly more of their lives outdoors in nature who were also the soldiers with the highest success at spotting IEDs (improvised explosive devices) and ambushes. This kind of awareness is common among birds and animals, but somehow most humans are the odd ones out.

And yet as human beings, we are also gifted. We are able to see revealed in nature the constant hand of the Divine Creator—if only we could remember how. We may remember also that we're tasked with the staggering responsibility of caring for the Creation, the *process.* This charge, to care for nature, is given as the primary purpose of humankind in one of the creation stories (Genesis 2:15). It is both a practical and a spiritual task.

To put all of this together is no easy challenge—to experience nature as process and relationship, to participate with nature, to discern how to care for it in harmony with its Creator—but that is the ethical and practical challenge at the heart of Forest Church. Where to start?

Have you ever asked a natural space for its permission for you to enter? I've seen the idea incorporated into Druid rituals and ecotherapy interventions. I'm not necessarily suggesting that you try it in exactly those terms, but there is value in pausing before you enter a wild area to put yourself in the right frame of mind; slow down, open yourself up to the possibility of participating respectfully, and ask for God's help in aligning your spirit with God's, uniquely active in the environment you're about to enter.

Between every two pines is a doorway to a new world.
John Muir

It takes some practice so don't give yourself a hard time when you don't do this or can't overcome the separateness we're accustomed to. But do recognize that when we intervene in nature, to pick a flower or medicinal herb or some berries or mushrooms, we're partaking in a process initiated and continually sustained by God. God's Spirit in nature likes it when you notice; it's a form of worship. Accept in return the blessing that will come to your own spirit and soul.

John Muir expresses the magic of this moment:

A few minutes ago every tree was excited, bowing to the roaring storm, waving, swirling, tossing their branches in glorious enthusiasm like worship. But though to the outer ear these trees are now silent, their songs never cease. Every hidden cell is throbbing with music and life, every fiber thrilling like harp strings, while incense is ever flowing from the balsam bells and leaves. No wonder the hills and groves were God's first temples, and the more they are cut down and hewn into cathedrals and churches, the farther off and dimmer seems the Lord himself.

Long, blue, spiky-edged shadows crept out across the snow-fields, while a rosy glow, at first scarce discernible, gradually deepened and suffused every mountain-top, flushing the glaciers and the harsh crags above them. This was the alpenglow, to me the most impressive of all the terrestrial manifestations of God. At the touch of this divine light, the mountains seemed to kindle to a rapt, religious consciousness, and stood hushed like devout worshippers waiting to be blessed.

CHAPTER 4

DEVELOPING YOUR
WILD SIDE

What makes a good Forest Church facilitator? Part of the answer is a deepening participative connection with nature and a growing familiarity with reading the Second Book of God, both of which help develop your authenticity for the role. The bulk of this is achieved by turning knowledge into wisdom through experience: by time spent actually doing it. It certainly adds to your authenticity if you've tried out Forest Church activities before asking anyone else to.

You don't need to be planning to facilitate a group to use the ideas in this chapter, though; they are just as relevant if you simply want to deepen your walk with God in nature, even if you have no intention of facilitating a Forest Church. In fact, to make the most of this chapter, forget about any groups for now; just think about what's right for you. Where is your journey leading? Where is God calling you? This chapter is full of suggestions to encourage you to develop your own nature connection practice.

Ask yourself: In what ways might you need to remedy your own nature deficit disorder, or get more flow into your life? Are you approaching any rites of passage, or do you have any spiritual direction needs that might harmonize with natural environments such as islands, mountaintops, coasts, or woodland? Nature, and these iconic places, can reach us viscerally; they mirror our inner worlds and take us farther than other self-reflection exercises. For example, standing on a hilltop in a brisk wind is a good place to imagine opening your hands and letting God carry away your concerns while giving you a fresh perspective; pick up a handful of leaves and then watch them fly away in the wind. Likewise, islands are good for isolation, for stepping away from your life, if that's what you need; so called blue-green walks (shore or river walks) are good for well-being . . . and so on.

It is better to do a little bit of nature connection every day than to plan a great expedition you might not get around to doing. With no hesitation, do something, anything, today, now. Go outside and take three mindful breaths right now. (Disregard this instruction if you're in a plane or submarine.) Well-being accumulates through daily nature connection, not the occasional two-week trip. Attempt to balance each and every day, rather than a year. The pertinent question is: what do you need to do *today* to connect with nature and God?

Experience—and reflection on your experience—will be your biggest teacher. An old saying from monastic wisdom advises: *Return to your cell and your cell will teach you everything.* In the context of this chapter, you could substitute "your cell" with the word "nature."

Basic Activities and Routines

The easiest and best place to start is to simply do more of what you already do: incorporate nature connection into your existing activities—your commute to work, your lunch breaks, daily errands, and so on. You don't need to be out in wilderness to connect to nature; if you're in the middle of a city, you're not far from nature, even if all you can see are the clouds. It is really a matter of being aware and mindful of the opportunities, many of which will be simple and informal.

What follows is a short list of accessible activities that form the most important scaffolding for nature connection and a deepening ability to read the Second Book of God. They also help develop authenticity as a Forest Church facilitator. Later in the chapter are some more extreme suggestions and some ideas about how to put these ideas into some sort of plan (or rule), in harmony with nature.

Sit Spot: I first came across the notion of a *"Sit Spot"* from Jon Young's book *Coyote's Guide to Connecting with Nature.* My interpretation of the activity is to visit, as often as you can, the same spot in nature, where you simply sit in silence and observe, listen, and smell (and sense with less conventional senses too). It may take you a bit of trial and error to find the right place. Ideal locations are ones with plenty of greenery growing at different layers (ground cover, shrubs, and trees) with enough biodiversity to allow insects, birds, and even animals to use them too. It could be your garden or a wilder corner of a local park as long as you'd feel safe being there. Jon Young, a master tracker and bird language expert, says that his "Sit Spot" in the forest near his New Jersey home had more to do with his development as a human being, not to mention as a naturalist, than anything else.

It is a deceptively simple practice that allows you to participate with nature—especially the parts with fur and feathers, who will slowly come to accept your presence. But it is also a place for connection with the ever-present Divine Spirit in nature, a place for contemplation and meditation, sometimes on what is happening around you, and other times on what you've brought with you. It won't take long for you to begin to generate alpha brain waves in this site, so you might find that it is a good activity for creativity and insight, although these aren't the main reasons for doing it.

Sunrise and sunset are good times, as is springtime generally. Some people take a small handful of split sunflower seeds to sprinkle nearby to further encourage the birds. Above all, the Sit Spot routine is a way to join in with the rhythms of nature. Before long, you realize that you are an integral part of the process. Also try it if you're somewhere other than your home turf, away on vacation, traveling for work, or even just out for a walk.

Journaling: You could call this routine a nature diary. I know that journaling is a common activity suggested in many developmental processes, from creative pursuits to spiritual direction and self-help. If you've come across it before, you'll no doubt remember how it was presented as a vital and crucial element of your development—and you'll no doubt be feeling guilty about not doing it . . . and annoyed with me for bringing it up again. What can I say?

If you've never made a practice of journaling before, let me assure you that it is a vital and crucial element of your development in nature connection. Get yourself a decent all-terrain notebook, ideally without lines and big enough for you to make sketches. Take it with you when you go out and about, and use it to capture notes, observations, thoughts, ideas, and drawings. Bring it back with you, and then do the same from the comfort of your armchair in the evening to reflect on your experiences. If I've spent any time in nature to deliberately connect and participate, I'll make some general notes, but I'll also make three headings for **Awe, Study,** and **Meaning**, and then use my journal to capture anything that's relevant to those categories. If nothing leaps to your mind, a good discipline is to find something to say anyway. This will help you to develop what might be a weak strand in your spiritual practice.

Overall, journaling is a bit like meditation: if you get into the habit, you'll find that it becomes self-sustaining. If you've ever read the nature notes in a newspaper—which can be beautiful pieces of poetry and prose—a good nature journal can develop into something similar. And don't feel you need to confine yourself to written notes; you can photograph, video, or record notes on a recording device or turn them into a blog, podcast, or vlog.

Study: Learning about what interests you most in the natural world happens easily on your own; as discussed in chapter 2, the farther you develop your area of passion, the less likely it is to be of interest to those around you. Having explored the idea of Study as it relates to reading the Second Book of God, I won't say a great deal about it here other than to highlight its importance in developing your wild side. Turning knowledge into wisdom through experience makes you a better facilitator, but you need to have the knowledge there in the first place.

Nature is school-mistress, the soul the pupil;
and whatever one has taught or the other has learned,
has come from God —the Teacher of the teacher.
Tertullian

My primary sources of Study materials are books on conventional naturalist subjects, from trees and fungi to more specialist material on tracking, natural navigation, weather lore, and even a book about the history of UK hedges. I also have books on pilgrim routes, natural theology, nature deficit disorder, eco-therapy, group dynamics, outdoor play, Druidry, and translations of writings by mystics who were particularly in tune with the natural world. To a lesser degree, I also learn from TV programs. The Internet is a great source of information, and YouTube is useful for practical information. Among my YouTube bookmarks are films that show the right knots to tie up a shelter and techniques for building cob ovens.

More traditional sources of education are also possibilities. It's not difficult to find courses on all sorts of related subjects. Some, offered by your local community college or other community education groups, may even be free. In the last month I've attended a talk on small-scale hydro power, a guided walk with an outstanding mycologist (both of which were free), and a three-day landscape reading course with the UK guru on the subject, Patrick Whitefield.

(Awe and Meaning, the other ways to read the Second Book of God, which are well covered elsewhere in this book in ways that are applicable to an individual's development, should be considered equally important as Study.)

Going out on your own: You'll find treasures to experience when you're with the other-than-human world . . . without other humans. When you're out and about, with time to explore, wander, and stop, it is easier to follow the inquisitive, playful thread of the moment when you're by yourself.

Nature connection and participation happens through your senses, but once the connection is made, it becomes internal, instinctive, almost introverted. Your attention can be balanced between your outer senses and the feeling of your inner spirit or energy, all the while in contact with, even at one with, the Spirit and energy around you. That balance is easier to maintain when you're not distracted by others' presence.

Extroverts, who depend on processing their ideas externally, may find this difficult, but odd as it might seem, you can fall into quite enlightening verbal conversations with elements you find in the natural world. In which case, being by yourself is a necessity. (More on this exercise later.)

You may be able to maintain a state of inner solitude even while being with other people, as long as you—and they—are comfortable with the normal conventions being put to one side. You need to be with others who understand and want to do the same thing; telling a companion who doesn't understand that you want to stop talking for the next hour might not go down well.

Giving thanks: You can't shift along the scale from *dominator of nature* toward *participant with nature* without appreciating more of our dependence on nature. Expressing gratitude formally, or simply acknowledging it informally, is an anchor to the humility and respect of participation. Giving thanks more often is a practical way to move further toward the participative, ethical dimension. Furthermore, psychological research indicates that giving thanks regularly builds and sustains well-being.

When you're somewhere beautiful, open to awesome and transcendent moments, you can quite easily discover and express thanksgiving for God's grace. That may even develop into the most heartfelt song of worship you've ever sung. At other times you might want to make thanksgiving a more deliberate exercise. It could form part of your journaling, or something you say as you leave your Sit Spot or as you cross the threshold from nature back into your home or work life.

To keep the exercise fresh, vary when and how you do it. Try something for a while, like writing your thanks in your journal, and then move on to another way of giving thanks, such as a simple prayer, a mini-ritual, or even having a go at writing a psalm (see chapter 6).

More Extreme Activities

By this I don't mean extreme sports (although some extreme sports are in fact good nature-connection activities). I'm talking here about activities that require a bit more dedication or planning. Some take you further into nature connection and others are useful skills to pick up as a potential group facilitator. The basic activities and routines described already form a Forest Church's core foundation, while the example activities that follow are presented simply to tempt you further.

Wild camping: This is an extension of the practice of being on your own in nature, and it allows you to go that much deeper into the connection simply because you're spending longer in the environment. You'll need camping equipment: shelter of some kind and a sleeping bag. Shelter can range from something you build woodcraft style to bivi bags, tarpaulins, or little tents. I use a very lightweight hiker's tent that opens along its length to give a similar experience to being under a tarp, which means I can leave the sides down in all but the worst weather and remain in contact with the environment around me. Wild camping in the United States isn't a legal right everywhere and camping laws vary from state to state, but national forests are considered public lands, which means that anyone can enter, visit, hike, and camp as long as camps are built at least 300 feet from any nearby road, trail, or body of water. The United States also has a number of "free campground" guides, which list secluded and little-known sites where it is legal to camp. Check online. Do some research into your specific area first. You can also find quiet and discreet paid campsites that offer almost the same kind of isolation.

Woodcraft and wilderness survival: These are popular these days, and there are plenty of sources of information. You're never far from a course, book, website, or TV program. I'm no expert, so I can't add very much more, but they are great opportunities for nature connection and provide lots of material for Study.

Pilgrimage routes and long-distance paths: If you travel to Europe, you'll find pilgrim routes winding their way along coasts, over mountain ranges, and through cities. In the United States, hiking all or some of the Appalachian Trail has become a sort of natural pilgrimage for many people. Pilgrimages are another obvious way to extend your nature connection time, but there is something to be said for undertaking them with others. You may prefer to take a long walk on your own, however, if it makes it easier for you to remain open to participating and being in dialogue with nature.

Pilgrimage routes, especially through densely sacred land such as the UK, very much involve the human story and our interactions amid nature. This is where landscape reading and sensing can be particularly interesting as you work out what it was about the place that first called humans to make it sacred.

Pilgrimage destinations that feature great monasteries, Roman remains, and stone circles may be interesting, but they have more to do with people who dominated nature than those who participated with it. The great monasteries were the giant agribusinesses of their time, and the Romans left partly because they over-exploited the soil. Interestingly, very little remains of the Celts and Druids who came after the stone-circle-building peoples and before the arrival of the Romans. Almost as a backlash against the nature-dominating practices of earlier times, it seems the Celtic people had a much subtler and less interventionary impact on the landscape—which is a bit more in the spirit of Forest Church. The Celtic Christians, of later centuries, are associated with some of the most breathtaking and beautiful wild locations that seem inspired by a more direct, sacred relationship with nature as God's creation.

My interest is primarily in the place itself rather than what we think its early inhabitants did or thought. This information, if we have it, is valuable and illuminating, but we need to relate directly with a place and the Divine Spirit, the *Anima Loci* that is there, afresh for our own times. This is no easy feat, as we're less practiced at it, but I'd rather read a landscape as a Druid or Celtic saint did than read what they wrote about it. In any case, perhaps the focus of a pilgrimage or long-distance path should be on the journey rather than the destination.

In North America, the First Nation peoples have also always had a direct experience of the sacred found in nature. First Nation sacred sites are, according to Indian rights activist Suzan Harjo, "lands and waters where people go to pray," some of which are geological formations, such as Bear's Lodge/Devil's Tower in Wyoming, while others are entire landscapes, such as the Black Hills of South Dakota or the Indian Pass trails that span hundreds of miles from southern California to the Mexican border. These sacred places are found on reservations, public lands, and private lands, but many of the most visible and well-known sites are on public lands, especially in the West. Visiting these locations can be a deeply spiritual experience, a form of pilgrimage. As outsiders to this spiritual tradition, however, we should always show respect for Native tribes and nations by obeying tribal laws and never intruding on private ceremonies.

Growing your own, permaculture style: Along the cutting edge of our attitudes toward nature lies our awareness of the connection between nature and our physical survival. Not just our food comes from nature but also our shelter and clothing and building materials, our medicine and fuel. Without the natural world we would literally not survive.

Attempting to grow some of your own food is a good way to increase your awareness of your dependence on nature—but I'm not talking about an annual vegetable garden of spuds, carrots, and peas. Instead, I'm suggesting that you create a forest garden: a permanent, perennial, no-dig ecosystem. Traditional annual vegetable gardens, such as your average backyard plot, don't so much work with nature as attempt to control it. Bare soil doesn't really occur in nature; if a tree comes down, exposing bare soil, or there is a landslide or flood, succession kicks in very quickly. The annuals (which are what most traditional vegetables are) get only this one chance to colonize the space, which is why they're quite rare in natural ecosystems. What the land really wants to be is woodland, and as humans, we spend much of our time and resources working against nature to keep it in the first stage of succession. A forest garden, on the other hand, works with nature (and it's possible even in a small area). It mimics the ecosystem of a young woodland, with plants growing at every layer, from roots and ground cover to canopy trees and climbers. Our intervention involves choosing plants that are useful to us (food, medicine, fuel, fiber, dye, etc.) and useful to the system (nitrogen fixing or mineral accumulating, for example), so that the system doesn't require any external resources (which are usually carbon costly). This method of horticulture has the apt nickname of "lazy gardening" because it requires very little maintenance.

A permaculture approach to growing your own food (or designing the whole system of your life's inputs and outputs), doesn't mean only a forest garden, but I'm suggesting it because it is a system of food production that sits between the food gatherers and food producers discussed in chapter 1. It is not a million miles away from the Garden of Eden—you may just find God walking there too.

Animal forms: Did a preschool teacher ever instruct you to curl up like an acorn and then slowly grow into a tree to be blown around by the wind? This is a common activity in UK play-schools. As a physical theater student in my early twenties, I also spent a great deal of time exploring the movement characteristics of natural elements such as water, air, and fire, all as ways to give depth to performances.

What can the practice of mimicking the movements or energy of animals teach us? Animal forms have a number of traditional applications, from hunting preparation and practice to movement forms such as yoga and Tai Chi. In the context of Forest Church, however, I can see two main reasons for exploring this.

The first is that animal forms might have a place in the wider concept of embodying our prayers and meditations. Making our spiritual thoughts physical is one way to bridge the gap between a head-based internal discipline and one that moves and uses the same physical language as nature. For example, practicing Tai Chi in a natural setting is a good way to explore and connect with the energy of the place. It is a way to widen our vocabulary and our understanding of nature and Spirit.

The second reason for mimicking animal forms has to do with our search for Meaning when reading the Second Book of God: to understand something, don't just think about it—be it, embody it. At an introductory level, this is as simple as playing games such as Fox Walking (described in chapter 6): walking through a woodland without making a sound by mimicking the delicate footsteps of a fox.

Wandering: More often than not, when we go into nature we're going with an agenda, to go for a walk from point A to point B. On the other hand, simply wandering, slowly, allows us to open to the lessons nature might want to teach us or the Awe God may want us to experience. Wandering is not the same as being aimless; instead we are moving with our minds present and our senses open, with a playfulness similar to what I call *vacation rules*. When you're on a vacation, you're not in a hurry, you're not needing to be productive or make the most of the time. A fuller version of yourself is present, and you're able to be steered by delight.

Pick an environment where you have permission to roam and where it is safe. You could head for somewhere you know well, but new locations where you've never been can add interest. You could even go somewhere you wouldn't normally choose to go to. If you always go to mountains, head instead to the lowlands, deserts, or wetlands.

One possibility, not for the inexperienced or faint-hearted, is to allow wandering to lead to getting lost. The very notion may fill you with fear brought on by visions of ending up as an undiscovered corpse, but it can be a bit more controlled than that. Perhaps start with getting lost within a small area you do know well—or by not looking at your map or compass as often as you would normally. A great suggestion from Matthew Arnold, facilitator of East Midlands Forest Church, is to set a start point, bring a GPS, and use the GPS only if you really need to. You could combine the exercise with the Study of natural navigation, wild camping, and the following activity.

Conversing with nature: When I first moved to the relative wilds and isolation of Mid Wales and the Cambrian Mountains, I began to explore the hills around our home, seeking out fascinating features in the landscape. Certain places called me, attracted me; some places I could see from my regular walks and others only from maps. One such trip was to a gorge at the head of a river, inaccessible by road and surrounded by forest and moorland. An eight-mile mountain bike trip along forestry tracks would take me to within a half-mile of it; the rest I'd have to figure out when I got there. But the point of the story isn't what I found (which was spectacular and memorable); the point is the awareness I experienced of the attraction and pull from a deep soul level to elements of the natural world. The exploration of that attraction can become a dialogue, and, odd as it might seem, these conversations with an element of nature such as a tree or rock, a waterfall or bird can be illuminating, surprising, and enriching. I had a conversation with the hidden canyon, after I'd recovered from the Awe of the place. In my conversation, it seemed polite to mostly listen, and what it had to say was so very slow and deep that I think I'm still waiting for it to finish its first sentence.

Allow the idea that a conversation might occur to be present in the back of your mind any time you're out wandering or are seeking nature-based spiritual direction. Wait until something calls you, and then give it your full attention. Giving something your full attention is one of the most loving and respectful acts you can offer. Since this is an element of nature, you will need to give it your attention primarily through your senses. When it feels right, begin your dialogue. You can communicate conventionally through spoken language or through whatever mode suits you: song, movement, sounds, mime. Tell it anything and everything—whatever is on your mind —and then listen to the reply.

You might discover your conversation is similar to one you might have with a friend, where you discover you are understood, mirrored, and affirmed, but you may instead be challenged by a conversation that reveals a vulnerability or a need for healing and strengthening. There is a neat theory in psychology called *social prosthesis,* which suggests that we find in our friends, particularly those who are different from us, emotional or cognitive strengths to augment a perceived weakness in ourselves. In some ways our sense of self can be extended to include those elements of other people to make us more whole or balanced. I suggest that something similar can happen with nature in which you'll find mirrored every element of your soul and every element of God's eternal power and Divine nature.

We're comfortable with the idea that a particular natural environment might refresh and sustain us; this is simply exploring that connection in more depth. A further extension of this idea of attraction and dialogue with something we might encounter in nature is at a spiritual level. It seems to many people that elements in nature, a mountain or a tree, for example, have a distinct spirit about them, a personality. Some would go further and attribute a living soul—a god— to these elements, plants, objects, and natural phenomena, a belief system which is called *animism*. (I can understand the thinking behind this because I have an unfriendly cockerel that I'm sure is possessed by something.) But animism doesn't sit comfortably within the Christ Tradition. Instead, we might entertain the idea of *panentheism,* which describes one God who created the universe but also comes into it, inhabits it, and interacts with it. We can know the Divine Spirit only in part, as Spirit expresses different aspects in different places and things.

This is, however, only a simple starting point to attempt to connect experience with Christian theology. Some people would add fasting to the activity of conversing with nature and/or wandering. Fasting is a way of preparing and opening yourself up to connection to God through nature, but it is also an embodied act, a spiritual discipline that happens in nature's language. The best way to see if this is something that works for you is to try it.

Outdoor qualifications: You may already have some relevant qualifications such as first-aid training, but that's just the start. You may be motivated to go farther and do more coursework. If you have the time, budget, and motivation to head down this route, it will hugely benefit your Forest Church group, especially if you want to do related activities with your group. In the United States, the Wilderness Skills Institute, a training partnership between the Appalachian Trail Conservancy, the United States Forest Service, and the Wilderness Society, offers two-week programs in various aspects of wilderness training (www.trailcrews.org/wilderness-skills-institute). In Canada, organizations such as AMARUK (www.amaruk.com/gopro) offer training programs in wilderness skills. Programs like these are designed to prepare you for the possible dangers of wilderness areas in North America—but even if all you're doing is wandering round a park with a coffee shop at the end, some first-aid and outdoor safety training can be really useful.

Start a whole new life: Ask yourself where in nature you feel closest to God—and then sell your current home and move there. Live off the land and use wood fuel to stay in touch with nature's rhythms. Generate your own power, walk into the hills or along the coast or go sailing (if that is what does it for you). As a life coach, I found that almost everyone has her own big wish, and that she just needs a series of steps to turn her dreams into reality. I've seen what is possible in other people's lives, and I have made the leap myself (but that is a whole other story).

COMING UP WITH A PLAN

Before setting off on your own journey of development (incorporating some of these suggestions, the basic activities earlier in the chapter, and your own ideas), you might want to explore two different starting points: delight and discipline. It all depends on whether you're motivated more by the carrot or the stick. If you're a self-starter and really enthusiastic about the prospect of getting out and deepening your nature connection, that is a great motivation if it translates into action. For many people, however, the busyness and pressure of life can crowd out the good intentions of setting aside time to be in nature. It's an elephant-and-rider thing; the rider can see the value in setting aside time for the activities but the elephant needs a little discipline to stay on track. A plan might help.

Making action plans is an essential element of reflective practice, which is how adults learn and develop. Reflective practice is the cycle of *planning, action, observation,* and *reflection,* leading back into planning. Journals are a good way to do the planning and reflection aspects. Good action plans are positive, concise, specifically defined, and dated. The success of many endeavors was built on this method, but it isn't for everyone.

The first plan you could devise is a description of where you'd like to be in a year's time: places to have visited, Study to have completed, and so on. An easier way to start might be to limit your goal numerically or by a period of time. For example, it might be better to set out to learn to identify five native trees rather than fifty. Or if you've always wanted to paint directly from nature, decide on a manageable goal, such as three small canvases, rather than aiming to fill a gallery. Another sensible way to limit yourself is to try something for a short period of time. If, for example, your plan is to spend half an hour at a Sit Spot every day, do it for a month rather than commit to doing it forever.

A final strategy is to combine nature connection with something you're already doing. For example, if you love photography, you could combine it with capturing a number of Study subjects, such as plants or animal signs or weather phenomena (whatever you're motivated to learn about). If you love walking, try a pilgrimage route, or you could combine visiting friends with visiting sacred sites. Foraging began for me when we had walked every last route near where we were living and wanted a different experience. I now combine identifying edible plants with any short walking commute or waiting time outside. Many nature connection activities are a good antidote to boredom, since many of them are potential flow activities.

Following Nature's Rhythm

Your eventual pattern of nature connection activities—your own rule, if you like—could follow nature's rhythm; the two are crying out to go together. So much of nature is its patterns and phases. (These rhythms are part of the process of nature highlighted in chapter 3.)

If you live in an urban environment and you don't have anything to do with your own food production, these passing seasons may touch you only lightly, but you may be missing important lessons. The remedy can't always be a move into the country to grow-your-own, so you may have to make more of a conscious effort to stay in tune with these patterns despite the insulating effect of city life.

In relation to our own lives, the three greatest rhythms in nature are night and day, the lunar (synodic) months, and the solar patterns dividing a year into the quarters between solstices and equinoxes. There are many more patterns (such as the carbon and water cycles), but these three have most relevance to our own rhythms.

The lunar months are irregular, since they follow a different pattern every year. They're somewhat awkward to fit into what is supposed to be an easy pattern, so instead, begin working with a daily and quarterly rhythm.

I'm not going to suggest the specific elements for a rule, which lies outside the scope of this book, but I will give some detail to the seasonal elements to inspire you when devising your own pattern. To begin with, the year neatly falls into two halves.

The Light Half: This part of the year falls between the spring and autumn equinoxes (March 21/22-ish to September 21/22- ish in the northern hemisphere; the dates are reversed for the southern hemisphere), six months of the year when the day length is longer than the night. This is the half of the year for new life and growing, beginning with the hope and promise of seed sowing in the spring and ending with a time of resolution and fulfillment during harvest in the autumn.

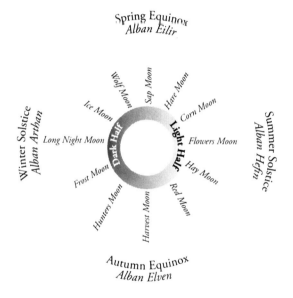

*An extra moon in any month is called the *blue moon*.

This half of the year is an easy time to be outside. The warmer, lighter summer months make it possible to camp and celebrate and enjoy nature. A lot is happening in the natural world during these months. Many plants flower, enabling easier identification. Plants grow the most, converting sunlight into matter. Birds mate, build nests, and raise broods. These are perfect months for the beginner naturalist.

Daily (or regular) activities during the light half of the year could include visiting a Sit Spot, journaling, tending a garden, and practicing weather lore.

This period is split into two quarters by the summer solstice. The first quarter, from around March 21 to around June 21, is a time of promise with patience. Due to the thermal lag in the earth's warming, days in March and April can seem icy as the ground holds on to winter's cold, but steadily the temperatures rise and the last frost will fall some time in April or May, depending on your location. During this quarter, nature is waking up and preparing. Molehills indicate that the ground has warmed up enough for earthworms to come to the surface. It's time for growing.

This period can further be split into three moons, if it is useful for you to work with these divisions for your own pattern. The names for these moons are traditional and resonate most with people working on the land; you may prefer to come up with your own names for these moons that have more relevance to your own relationship with nature and its cycles. You will need a chart specific to the year to tell you when the moons will be.

A full moon at the end of March is known traditionally as the Worm, Crow, or Sap Moon, echoing what is happening in nature. (You could use these names as inspiration for some relevant activity for the duration of that lunar cycle.) The full moon in April is the Egg, Hare, Grass, Seed, or Waking Moon. In May is the Milk or Corn Moon, and in June is the Honey, Flowers, or Mead Moon. An extra moon in any quarter is called the Blue Moon.

The second quarter of this light half, from summer solstice to autumn equinox, is really what we call summer. This quarter, even though it has the same amount of sun as the previous quarter, contains the hottest months. It is a time for activity, growth and harvest, a good time to undertake any major outdoor expeditions such as camping, pilgrimage, or celebrations. The full moons in this period are July's Hay or Thunder Moon; the Corn, Grain, Red, or Dog Moon in August; and the Harvest Moon in September, which takes us up to the equinox on the 21/22-ish (depending on the year) and the coming of the dark half.

The Dark Half: This part of the year contains awesome highlights for many people. Crisp, sunny days are like jewels amid displays of autumn leaves, log fires, snow, and yule celebrations. Nature is still; this is a time to pause, a time of preparation and rebirth. Being outside requires more care and a few more layers of clothing. If your work is on the land, you will have more time during this half for other nature connection activities.

Daily (or regular) activities during this half still involve visiting a Sit Spot, perhaps less often than before. It's a good time for planning and any structural work involved in gardening and food production. This is also the time for pruning and tree work. You can make use of the longer nights; if your sky is free from light pollution, this is a good time for stargazing. Best of all, these cold, dark months are a good time for Study if your subject involves reading or other forms of research and learning. I like to save up books on nature or other Forest Church subject matter to read over the winter.

Nature is still active in the last few months of the year. The quarter between autumn equinox and winter solstice feels busy, and just as the warmest summer months occur after the solstice, the coldest winter months happen in the following quarter, meaning that the autumn months (October, November, and December) still have some relative warmth. Gradually, however, this time becomes more reflective. Birds move south, out of your area, while others may come into your area from farther north. One essential experience for me during this time is to watch a murmuration of starlings, those aerial ballets when the flocks of birds fly and turn as one. Sunrise is later—and thus easier to catch—during the winter equinox than the summer. October has the Hunter's Moon, November has the Frost Moon, and December the Long Night Moon.

The second quarter of the dark half of the year falls between the winter solstice and the spring equinox. The sun is low, the day length starts to increase, and yet the earth holds the cold. Nature is waiting, preparing. These months are good for landscape reading, especially after heavy frost or light snow, which can highlight frost pockets and micro-climates. It's obviously a good time for planning activities for the coming lighter half of the year, but I find myself outside almost as much as in the summer. Nature is too good to miss, and if there is snow, we don jackets and gloves, and go out and make the most of it. January has the Ice Moon and February the Wolf Moon.

EQUIPMENT

The most important equipment doesn't weigh anything: it's wisdom carried in your head (so say the woodcraft teachers). Resist the temptation to buy loads of the latest outdoors stuff, becoming a consumer for its own sake; cool as some of it is, it's not really in the spirit of Forest Church. I recommend you spend time in nature first and let your specific experience suggest what equipment you *need*.

Backyards and parks are perfectly fine for nature connection, but if you're heading into the wild, some items are worth getting, such as good boots and a decent jacket (although one of my group prefers his "wellies" to anything more expensive). I favor outdoor clothing and waterproofs made from natural materials in natural colors. These are as effective as the synthetic alternatives, but they don't rustle or look like neon; blending in is all part of participating with nature.

If I'm out for a day, I also take water, sometimes food, a first-aid kit, a map (which is useful only if you know how to read one), and a bag to put it all in. And depending on what I'm doing, I'll take the relevant equipment or books. I often have a phone with me, but I don't rely on getting a signal. And I usually have a small notebook or a larger sketchbook if I think I might be in the mood to stop and draw or write.

Other equipment is occasionally useful. A camera is sometimes good to have if it doesn't interrupt moments of Awe (see chapter 2). If I'm identifying plants and foraging, a botanist's loupe and containers for the harvest are useful.

In an effort to travel light, I must confess to being a fan of various smart-phone apps. Whatever the downsides are (I can hear you drawing in breath through barely parted lips, given what I've said above), the upsides are that I can take a lot of really good reference materials such as a key to all the fungi I'm likely to see (the book version is prohibitively heavy), a notebook, a camera, a GPS, detailed information about the geology beneath my feet, a theodolite, a planetarium, the Internet with links to sites such as www.pfaf.org, an offline OS Landranger map—and a phone, all of which fits in a pocket.

So now we've laid the foundation. In natural terms, we might say instead that we've planted the tree. Now it's time to grow the branches.

CHAPTER 5

GROWING YOUR OWN
BRANCH OF FOREST CHURCH

All you need to set up a Forest Church is a group of people
and some nature. Unlike setting up other new groups, it isn't
difficult to find a venue for a Forest Church. There's something that's likely to be available, and it doesn't cost anything.
Your style can be unique; there isn't a prescribed model.

You may want to start a Forest Church as a regular
stand-alone group, or you may already be involved with an
existing church and want to host Forest Church gatherings.
You might want to run a one-off nature-based quiet day or
a longer retreat. You could use the ideas and activities for a
youth group.

Some groups meet once a month at the same park for an
hour and a half. Other groups meet for an evening ritual or
ceremony on the eightfold Celtic wheel of the year in someone's back yard. Some groups meet in rural and mountainous areas; others meet in city parks and green spaces. Some
groups structure what they do quite rigidly, while others are
far less structured. Many of the groups are open to anyone
from any spiritual background and particularly attract those
from Earth Spiritualities.

I'm part of Mid Wales Forest Church. We started with a pattern of meeting on the third Sunday of every month, somewhere different each time. We rotate between three sorts of gatherings. On the four Sundays closest to the equinoxes and solstices, we have a shared meal and some kind of ritual or ceremony to mark the season. The next month, we go on a walk, which will include moments to pause for site-specific meditations. The month after that we run a workshop or activity of some kind. The workshops often introduce a Study subject, such as tree identification, forest gardening, foraging, or tracking, which are popular with new people, but workshops can also introduce techniques related to Awe (such as mindfulness walking exercises) and Meaning (such as psalm writing).

FORMING A CORE GROUP

If you're thinking of starting a Forest Church, it may be tempting to imagine what the group might be like fully formed and launch with something as close to that as possible. For example, your ambition might be to run events for about thirty people, open to anyone from any background, and you might try to make your first event match that vision. In our experience, that would be a mistake, because what we're asking people to do in Forest Church is quite unusual and on the edge of some people's comfort zone. One alternative might be to take that same group of people through a gradual process of development, introducing deeper ideas and practical exercises as you go, but then it may be difficult for newcomers to join; the group may effectively be closed and function more like a course cohort.

A better process is to form a core group of people to act as holders and demonstrators of the vision and ethos of the group. If there are enough of these people present at your events, it makes it far easier for newcomers to join and feel comfortable participating without feeling self-conscious or silly.

My suggestion would be to see the development of your Forest Church as splitting into two stages: forming your core group and then opening your events up to a wider audience. It may be a two-year process or more to get to this second stage. There may be some blurring of the stages, depending on what sort of event you're putting on; for example, you can make Study-based workshops open to anyone and publicize them widely. At the opposite extreme, you may feel it is right to make your gatherings by invitation only, particularly your rituals, until your core group is established.

If you're new to an area, you may need to find your core group among those who come to your events. Until you have that experienced group in the middle, your events will have to be at an introductory level. Eventually, the core group may be eight to twelve people, with at least six present at any event.

Essentially, a core group member needs to *get* what your Forest Church is all about and be able to demonstrate that to other people. Forming a core group may be easy if you already know the right people, or it may be a process of maturing and developing individuals into the role.

A core group member needs to be strong—or at least be developing—in these three facets:

1. Followers of the Christ Tradition who are comfortable holding their faith sensitively among others from different paths.
2. Committed to deepening a participative relationship with nature, ethically and practically. (As explored in chapter 3, we all have some way to go in this area.)
3. Comfortable being demonstrative. Mostly, this means showing others how to do Forest Church during your events, which at times might mean

being playful and childlike. It also means positively and practically demonstrating points one and two through their actions, rather than relying on words to explain them.

The core group is a necessary feature of a *centered set,* which is a description of a group that demonstrates and holds its vision at its center but is open to anyone who might or might not hold similar ideas. Anyone joining the group may be at various distances away from the core vision or values and traveling toward or away from it—and they are welcome wherever they are on their journey.

The core group, or "vision bearers" as some Forest Churches call them, might meet separately to plan future events and may develop a role giving feedback to the facilitator, identifying strengths, weaknesses, and areas for development. They may ideally share some of the work involved in organizing, publicizing, and facilitating events or parts of events.

Once the core group is in place, the nature of your gatherings can change. If you haven't publicized them widely or opened them to the public, you might consider doing that now. If you've been open to all comers from the beginning, having a core group might allow you to take what you're doing to a deeper level.

It's worth emphasizing again that finding the perfect candidates is not easy, if possible. You'll likely need to do some development, training, and encouragement with them in one of the three facets described above.

PUBLICITY AND MARKETING

Most of us are from the film *Field of Dreams* school of marketing: *If you build it, they will come.* We're so positive and optimistic about what we're doing, we assume that lots of other people will feel the same way we do. More often than not, this is a mistake, and you can find that half your time, energy, and preparation goes into trying to get people to come to what you've organized. To put it another way, if you want to start a stand-alone, self-contained Forest Church, plan that half of your time, energy, and preparation will go into spreading the word and letting people know about your events, especially in the first couple of years.

A much longer book than this one would still only scratch the surface of how to do this most crucial aspect of your group's formation effectively. If you're not a natural networker or able to call on a wide list of contacts, you need to give this serious consideration—but be encouraged! Many people do instinctively like the idea of Forest Church. It has a lot going for it inherently, as suggested in chapter 1.

Five things we've found that work well when doing publicity are:

1. Collect a wide news distribution list, asking interested people for contact details. Use e-mail lists and events listings sites and tap into local networks that already exist in your area; do all the basics of spreading the news about your Forest Church.

2. Differentiate your message between those who have never heard about what you're doing, those who have heard but not taken part, those who have taken part once, and those who are regulars . . . and those who are enthusiastic fans. Each of these groups needs a different message.

3. If you have any enthusiastic fans, especially ones who are good networkers, encourage them to help spread news about your events.

4. Don't rely on social media. Encourage face-to-face conversations. They are much more effective.

5. Run workshops on popular naturalist or outdoor subjects. These are more attractive to newcomers than a sunrise ritual or day-long pilgrimage.

Be sensitive when using church networks. Avoid seeming like you're in competition with what they're doing.

What follows in the rest of this chapter is a whistle-stop tour of some of the skills and issues you might consider if you're wanting to facilitate a stand-alone Forest Church, particularly if you've no experience with anything similar. This might seem daunting to someone interested in Forest Church more casually, who just wants to run the occasional event—but don't let it put you off. It is a lot to remember, so concern yourself only with what's most relevant to you.

FACILITATION SKILLS

Why should Forest Church be *facilitated* rather than *led*? The distinction is not as black and white as that, since leadership skills and techniques are very much part of facilitation, but a facilitated group has the potential to do more than one that is just led, taught, or guided.

Two key ideas are fundamental to understanding group facilitation. First, a facilitator has only the group and its aims as his focus, which means that when facilitating, a person isn't accountable to a parent organization or governing body. Second, a facilitated group is different from a class or team, because it is able to reach a point of *synergy* when it is able to do more than the sum of its parts. More often than not, group decision making is done through cooperation rather than democracy or autocracy, and accountability and responsibility are shared.

Strictly speaking, when you're facilitating rather than teaching or leading, you don't get involved in content, you simply guide the group through a task. Quite often with

Forest Church events, you may use facilitation skills in combination with leading or teaching.

Facilitation is also about modeling behavior, so be relaxed and positive, and be yourself. Others will follow your lead.

Facilitating a group might sound attractive. You may even devote some time to reading up on or training in the relevant skills, only to discover with some frustration that groups can be more comfortable being led or taught rather than facilitated. Facilitation is a two-way dynamic, and groups of people expecting something else can change the dynamic to one that suits them better. Some events can feel like a teacher-and-student dynamic or even a tour guide with a group of tourists waiting to be entertained, which places a lot of responsibility on whoever is facilitating to *put on a good show.* The crucial aspect hidden in that dynamic is that it makes it easy for those attending to opt out of fully participating. This is understandable, since participating is demanding and exposing, but it is also the only place where change and depth of experience are found.

These issues can be handled by being a good facilitator, creating a space and dynamic that make it okay for people to step out of their comfort zones. Play is an example of one such space; if something is a game, then people are usually more willing to participate, since the unwritten rules of play-space allow them to act differently than normal. Your core group should help demonstrate the way.

As mentioned above, a good facilitator has leadership skills that allow him or her to provide focus, vision, and direction. Two models of leadership that are particularly valuable are the leader as *visionary* and the leader as *coach.* Being able to share and express the vision for Forest Church will be important to inspire people's transition from *interested* to *fully committed* participants. Sharing vision and inspiration is also a way to motivate other people to take action.

As a leader, your role is to help the group succeed in whatever it is doing—it is not to look for opportunities to bask in the glow of seeing yourself as important or have others recognize your authority. Keep your ego in check. Leadership may also emerge elsewhere within the group. You may appoint individuals as leaders for specific tasks or accept other people's offers to facilitate gatherings.

The *coaching* model of leadership includes a set of skills to encourage and enable other people to develop their own journey of transformation. Coaching is usually done one-to-one, rather than to the group as a whole. The coaching model is all about encouraging others to clarify their own ambitions and use their strengths to bring about change. You may use these skills to develop your core group, or you may find people attending your events who also want to develop their wild side away from the group. Coaching skills are also useful in nature-based spiritual direction.

A key coaching skill to develop is the art of asking questions. Some Forest Church Study-related events are concerned with sharing or imparting knowledge. Fact giving is appropriate when someone wants to know something and there is no way they could work it out or find out (or they'd get really frustrated trying to). Learning something might be the reason why people come to your Forest Church event, but seek a balance between giving facts and asking questions. If done well, this is a good way to raise curiosity and set someone off on her own journey of Study.

Learning and shared Study can be opportunities to empower other people, but they do unavoidably mean that someone has more knowledge than another, which is potentially dangerous territory. Holding more knowledge than those around you is a powerful position, and that power, if abused, can demean, disempower, and belittle other people. The task is to facilitate others to learn, not to enjoy the power of knowing more—and asking questions more often than providing facts is a good way to do that.

You can ask questions at different levels. Asking easy and introductory questions that are well within someone's comfort zone builds his confidence to learn more. Many people are quick to profess complete ignorance as a defensive measure—"I don't know anything"—and you can help them drop their defenses by starting somewhere easy. You can then go up a level and ask them a more taxing question that means they have to think things through a bit. Occasionally, you can go even farther and ask questions about things they didn't know you could know; if done artfully, you might even elicit an "Aha!" moment.

For example, if you were facilitating an introductory workshop on foraging, you might run across a healthy-looking elderberry bush along the edge of a field. Before telling the people in your group what the bush was, you could ask if anyone else knows, just in case someone does. Then, to take things one step further, you might ask if anyone knows what parts of the bush are edible. Most people have probably heard of elderberry jelly or elderberry wine, so start there. You then might discuss using the flowers to make fritters or the berries for medicinal tinctures. To take your questioning even further, into territory your group might never have considered, you could ask them what an elderberry bush indicates about the land or ask them how they could make an musical instrument from its branches. Because of its variety of uses, elderberry bushes were part of many early homestead plantings, growing alongside lilacs and forsythia, so its presence often indicates that the land was once an old farm. Its woody stems are easily hollowed, making them good for making flutes and whistles.

Remember, as the facilitator, the group is your focus. This means you go at the group's pace rather than your own.

With a core group in place, it may still take some time before you're able to experience group synergy, but when it is working well, you are facilitating internal and external processes for the group, the individuals in that group, and for yourself. You may get the best results if you keep your facilitation style light, positive, and playful, which works to people's strengths and encourages participation. But that's not to say that you can't invite or encourage strong emotions, even upsetting ones, and you should be prepared to offer a safe holding space for such reactions should they happen. For example, transcendent and Awe-inspiring moments do occur during Forest Church events, which can trigger turbulent reactions in some people. Or folks might get frustrated if they can't do a particular activity that others are finding easy.

As a good facilitator, you may want to consider intentionally taking people out of their *comfort zones* from time to time. Such excursions are . . . well, they're *uncomfortable,* but they can also be occasions of deep growth and insight.

Why is this? Think about the words you associate with being within your comfort zone: security, ease, stability, and relaxation are some that spring to mind. These are all positive qualities of comfort—but what about negative aspects, such as sameness, boredom, and stagnation? On the other hand, here are some of the words that might spring to mind when you think about being outside your comfort zone: discomfort, stress, uncertainty, fear, struggle, and vulnerability. But there are some significant positive ones too: challenge, adventure, excitement, learning, flow, and most important, change. Clearly, being within your comfort zone isn't all good—and there are great rewards to be found outside it.

To facilitate people outside their comfort zones, recognize that they might not like the experience; by definition, they're supposed to feel out of their depth and experience some stress. To make it easier, provide step-by-step plans for the activity that nudges them outside their comfort zones and offer regular feedback and encouragement. This will help them measure their progress and learning. Find a level of challenge that isn't so high it pushes them too far into something so intense that all they can do is survive.

Recognize that within your group is a mixture of introverts and extroverts (and some ambiverts who will opt to be introverts at first)—and when venturing outside of their comfort zones, introverts need particular treatment. Let them watch first; don't urge them to join in immediately. Don't demand immediate answers and give them time to think. If you need to teach them or provide feedback, do so one-to-one, and don't expect them to be as gregarious as extroverts. Remember that introverts will prefer to go deeply into one experience rather than experience lots of things at a more shallow level, as an extrovert might.

Another useful facilitation tip is to remember that you have different responsibilities to the *task,* the *group,* and the *individual.* This management model was invented by John Adair; he called it *action-centered leadership.* It is very difficult to satisfy all three elements, as their needs are often conflicting.

Years ago, when I led an eighteen-mile walk, in the first hour I could see that we had fallen off the pace, and some of the newcomers were struggling at the back, while others were asking for a break. I explained that if we didn't speed up, there was no way we were going to complete the walk on time, a statement which wasn't received with universal enthusiasm. As we continued, a good friend who happened to be a police trainer said to me that I was being *task* orientated rather than group focused or individual focused. She explained the model to me, which proved to be a helpful and timely conversation. I remember asking her how it was possible to satisfy all three responsibilities—and she replied that she'd never met anyone who could. Nevertheless, keeping this model in mind will help you analyze the problems that crop up during events. We finished the walk, as a group, a little late, with some individuals a bit tired and fed up, which was perhaps the best outcome we could have managed.

When you are focused on the *task,* your responsibilities are to create a plan in advance, identifying the resources, tools, and processes you'll need to do so—and then identify ways to measure your progress. At the start of the gathering you can explain the vision and purpose of the task to the group and define the activity and the schedule. (The latter will be very important to some individuals.) If, however, during an activity, you become too task orientated, you lose your presence and awareness of other important things, not least your openness to participating with nature.

Your responsibilities to the *group* are to set the soft tone, the style, culture, and approach. More formally, you can reiterate for the group the vision (for the event and for Forest Church). You can develop any teamwork and cooperation that might be necessary and monitor group morale and behavior. You'll need to reaffirm the objectives of the group and the task. As the group matures you can encourage synergy and hopefully encourage the group to jell as friends.

Your responsibilities to each *individual* are to recognize personal strengths, needs, aims, and fears and to support each person through her unique challenges. You can also give individuals responsibility, recognition, and praise where appropriate. During events, you'll need to facilitate a wide range of individual understanding, positive and negative affect, and buy-in with the core aims of Forest Church, such as participating with nature. As you can imagine, satisfying particular individual needs is quite an art. People arrive late, forget to bring things, don't wear appropriate clothing, fall ill, get tired, or otherwise create challenges you didn't predict. The responsibility of dealing with these issues can be shared among your core group. Make sure that some core group members are available to address some of the more derailing individual needs that might crop up. For example, quite often on walks we allow for a possible split so that a core group member will be able to take those getting tired or parents with children on a shorter route. You might think all this is not really relevant to the informal setting of Forest Church, but there is every possibility that you'll encounter all these challenges even during a one-off afternoon walk around a country park!

An issue for many individuals in a group has to do with language. So often it is the words we choose to use, especially when talking about God, that give people problems. If we use language that assumes other people share our world views, we run the risk of alienating some individuals. Referring to God solely as male, for example, is often a problem, as is using the word "we" when you mean "I." Saying, "We, your children, ask for your guidance, Father," may not strike you as problematic—but many individuals will have a problem with your choice of words. One solution is to only use gender-neutral language—for example, "God, who loves all his children," becomes, "God, who loves all God's children"—but that can become a bit clunky if overused. Another solution, instead of inclusive language, is to use creative and expansive language, using many ways to describe God, both male and female. The line could be reworded as, "Great Spirit, whose love excludes no one," which has more of a ring to it—and would allow individuals from other earth spiritualities to remain included. The word *God* can become Divine Spirit, Creator, Adonai, Great Spirit, Forgiving Father, Loving Mother, the Source of All, Divine Mystery, Eternal Spirit, Sevenfold Spirit. You can find inspiration from the natural features or phenomenon around you: God of the Vast Ocean, Spirit of the Mighty Beech, Master of the Running Deer. Be creative, be expansive. *Christian/Christianity,* which is a loaded word (even for Christians), can become, "Follower of Jesus," "Jesus

Tradition," or "Christ Tradition." I use the latter for theological and cosmological reasons that suit me, and I don't feel that I immediately alienate whoever I'm talking to by saying that I'm a follower of the Christ Tradition—whereas I might if I said I was a Christian.

While we're on the subject of language, why was "church" used in the name Forest Church? Isn't that as problematic? For some it is, and we took a long time to arrive at the name and decide that it was appropriate (the decision was shared). Reasons in its favor are that it does perfectly describe what we're doing but hopefully prompts a quizzical, smile-in-the-mind reaction; as *Forest School* is to normal school (wow, FOREST school?), so *Forest Church* is to normal church. After years of being very cautious in my descriptions of my own faith, so as to keep the conversation going, I felt here was something I could stand behind and nail my colors on it; here is a church that I long to be part of, that I feel authentically works, where I feel proud to invite other people who aren't from the Christ Tradition. Regardless, "Forest Church" rarely appears or is said on its own without further description that can clarify what it is.

To return to facilitation, many of the skills I've described are useful at the planning stage of Forest Church events, but really, you get to practice them only *during* events—and you won't always get them right—which is why reflective practice is useful if you want to learn and grow as a facilitator. Invite feedback at the end of events, but distinguish between feedback on content (what was said, what happened, feelings, ideas, reactions, etc.), and feedback on the process (timing, location, instructions given, length of breaks, etc.). I preempt some of this by inviting people at the beginning to tell me if they have suggestions to improve what we're doing as we go along; it's no good to find out at the end that someone couldn't hear or that we were going too fast.

More in-depth feedback might be appropriate from core group members and for longer events such as retreats or courses. Things that are often problems, both for individuals and for group synergy, can be related to power (personal, positional, factional, and knowledge wielding), talking too much and holding the floor (often men), language use (as mentioned above) and timekeeping (the perennial bane of group facilitators and the habitually-on-time folks).

The last thing to say to you as a facilitator is this: you have to be okay with people not liking what you do (or, if you can't be okay, find a way to manage your discomfort without it derailing you). If your interpersonal motivation is to be affiliative (wanting everyone to like you), then you can find that dominates your style and causes you stress as you try to please everyone. It is another good reason to carry out reflective practice, to be surer about the event you've put together and less emotionally turbulent about some people not liking you or what you've done. Friendly and supportive core group members can help too.

DEVISING MATERIAL

How do you put together a Forest Church event? Start with a big vision—what sort of group do you want to be part of?—and work backward from there.

You might add some detail to your vision by asking further questions. What does the group know? What do they do? How are they as a group toward each other and the wider community? In what ways do they give back to nature and what is their justice and peace agenda? How is your group a church? And how are you sustained in your role as facilitator?

Some activities, such as guided walks, quiet meditations, and working parties are fairly straightforward, as are workshops around naturalist-type subjects, as long as you or a group member has knowledge to share. Ceremonies and rituals take a bit more inventiveness and skill. They also flag an issue having to do with paper use. You might be perfectly happy holding paper and giving sheets to your participants for rituals and liturgy—but there's something about using tree products in that way that doesn't quite feel right to me personally. If you feel the same, you may want to find alternative ways of running rituals that limit the number of people who need words and make the responses simple to remember.

Inspiration for gatherings can come from your passions and interests, and from your own nature connection activities, including Study, books, and courses. When you get into the creative detail of devising a gathering and you have questions but no answers about certain aspects, you can put the advice found in chapter 1 into practice: put the problem down and go for a walk.

It isn't all up to you, though. Before long you'll discover in your group people who are experts on birds or native wild flowers, meditation or drumming, woodcraft, or the many possible walks around you. You can also bring in other people to lead sessions or you could follow, as a group, an outsourced study course.

When I'm devising an event or gathering, I'll choose a subject for which I have some interest and passion; that way I'll be more motivated to work on it and more enthusiastic when facilitating the event. First, I'll sketch out some rough ideas and then visit the location once or twice. While I'm there, I'll look for ways to make the activity site specific. I try to give myself time in the planning to allow inspiration (Awe) and the Spirit to work on deepening my understanding of the material.

In your preparation, be clear what the aims of the session are. It might be to help others learn something, or it might be to facilitate nature connection or to encourage people to drop their barriers. Aims for gatherings might also relate to a wider strategy, such as group bonding.

Look again at the ideas that define Forest Church, found in the introduction. Are you participating with nature? Have you left space for nature to contribute? Is there room for God to speak?

By way of inspiration, the final chapter of this book is a collection of ideas, activities, events, ceremonies, rituals, and prayers for you to use.

A final thought about material and facilitation is that you'll more than likely have to go at a pace somewhat slower than you (and a few core members) would like. For example, I'd love to be part of a group that wants to do some of the more extreme activities. I'd love to go wild camping for a weekend under tarpaulins or make a long pilgrimage—but it may be some time before there are others wanting to do the same things. Also, I bring in the bigger ideas and ethics behind Forest Church only when individuals are ready to receive them. A good number of people will likely come to your events who might simply categorize Forest Church as a fellowship group or as an interesting workshop about trees—which is fine. In time, however, you can see the effects that practically participating in nature begins to have. You create the space and tell the stories; let nature and God do the changing.

Earth or Nature-Based Religions

Most Forest Church groups are open to anyone. That is how a centered set operates, and many people will come who long to be part of a group-based spirituality that includes nature, but who don't fancy joining a Druid or Pagan group. Some people have simply been waiting for something in the Christ

Tradition to come along that doesn't look like the traditional model of church.

You may also build relationships with groups or individuals from other New Spirituality groups, which is really exciting and a great way to learn and share perspectives. You may have a lot to learn too.

When considering New Spiritualities such as Druidry, Heathenism, the various Pagan groups, and New Age groups, it is a mistake to view them as a homogeneous group. New Age groups are quite different, and they're viewed differently by the others. There is a spectrum within New Spiritualities between New Age at one end, which you could categorize as ethereal and Eastern influenced, in contrast to the Earth Spiritualities at the other end, which are grounded and more influenced by Western European practices, places, and ideas. (Many individuals from the informal New Age end of the spectrum, however, might not be aware of the distinction.) Forest Church sits at the Earth Spiritualities end of the spectrum, but attracts people from both ends.

Understanding specific New Spirituality groups and practices is a huge topic. If you're interested, you could explore the group as part of your Study, as some Forest Church facilitators are doing. I myself have studied with OBOD (Order of Bards, Ovates and Druids). Some Forest Church groups are attempting to welcome, and participate with (as authentically as possible) practicing Druids and Pagans. These groups hold ceremonies and gatherings where both Christ-followers and New Spiritualities can form a meaningful circle.

SAFETY AND RISK ASSESSMENT

For various reasons you may be motivated to get some formal qualifications such as outdoor leadership, advanced navigation, and first aid (or many others, depending on the type and terrain of your events), and you may consider getting insured for public liability. Whether you do or not, it is a very good idea to do a *risk assessment* before your event. For one thing, it encourages you to see the environment from a fresh perspective. This assessment generally follows a pattern similar to that shown in the table. Risk assessments can be more or less complicated than the table below indicates.

What is the hazard?	Who might be harmed and how?	What measures are you taking?	Who is responsible?
Low branches	Minor injury to anyone	Warn people before moving through the trees	FC Facilitator All adults
Poison ivy	Anyone could get minor to severe rashes	Avoid areas with lots of poison ivy. Be sure people can identify poison ivy and know to avoid it.	FC Facilitator
And so on ...			

Hazards can come from the site, the weather, the activity, and from other people. Common ones include:

- **Site:** low branches, briars, slippery slopes and surfaces, holes made by animals, barbed wire, stings, falling limbs from trees, falling dead wood, water (rivers, ponds, coast, etc.), uneven paths, animal dung, venomous snakes, dangerous animals, ticks, poisonous plants and mushrooms, extreme weather, debris in eyes from strong winds, and so on.
- **Group:** hypothermia, heat stroke, sunburn, dehydration, vulnerable individuals on their own,

pre-existing medical issues, phobias people forgot they have, medical emergencies, inappropriate clothing or footwear, no food or water, injury when lifting things, and so on.

- **Activity:** sharp tools, fire lighting, fire spreading, toxic fumes, falling off things, falling into water, improper use of equipment, equipment that's slippery in the rain, hot water, hot foods, and so on, depending on the activity.

Personally, I'd consider it a failure if worry over hazards stopped anyone from having a fun time or connecting with nature, so there is a balance to be found here.

QUESTIONS

Some questions might crop up when people are contemplating starting a Forest Church. Here are a few of the most common I encounter.

Does it cost anything?

No, it doesn't have to cost anything. Optional spending might be on some basic equipment, publicity, and insurance.

Do you charge people to attend?

I don't, but if we began to incur costs, I might make others aware of that if I couldn't cover the costs easily myself. A good motto is: Never resist an opportunity to be generous (or kind, wise, or loving, for that matter).

Is it a lot of work?

It depends what you want to get out of it. If you put effort into preparing yourself (see chapters 3 and 4) and your events (see chapters 5 and 6), you will be inadvertently telling the group that they are of worth as well as boosting your own confidence and authenticity.

Do I need to ask for anyone's permission?
You should never use private land without asking permission. You don't have to ask permission if you're using public parkland, but be sure you know and obey any additional rules having to do with fires, alcohol, dogs, and hours of entry. As far as the wider church goes, you don't need anyone else's permission, but it is a good idea to make friends with local leaders if you're operating on their patch.

Do I have to get liability insurance?
No.

Should I get liability insurance?
Ideally, but it depends somewhat on the events you're running.

Doesn't it appear to be a bit Pagan/Druid?
Hopefully!

What about the physically impaired?
The only answer is to best accommodate whoever wants to join. It is one of the reasons why the Mid Wales group varies what it does so that those with limited mobility, or toddlers too heavy to carry, can participate in the majority of events. When we do long walks, we build in a shorter route for those who want to take it and some events don't travel any distance at all.

Can people bring children?
Yes, but unless you have the resources and appropriately qualified individuals, children are their parents' responsibility at all times.

What is the ideal size for a group?
It depends on the event, but fifteen to twenty is a good number. Higher numbers are possible, but if you want to encourage any fellowship, you will need to subdivide the group.

Can you do it in the city?
Yes. Green spaces and countryside are never very far away.

Can you do it with people who have a low income?
Yes. We're from the Christ Tradition, so we'll find a way to make it work.

CHAPTER 6

EXAMPLE ACTIVITIES

This chapter contains a year's supply of activities (if you meet once a month), including meditative walks, rituals, workshops, exercises, and nature connection games. Some suggestions are tied to a time of year or a type of location, but most are flexible. Across the year, you'll find experiential activities designed to introduce the three ways into reading the Second Book of God from chapter 2: *Awe, Study,* and *Meaning.*

Alongside the months are the festivals of the eightfold Celtic year (those marked with an asterisk vary their dates). You may decide to follow this pattern rather than stick to a regular monthly gathering. However, if you meet on the third Sunday of every month, your events will be falling close to the four solar festivals, plus you have the benefit of a regular date.

Many of these examples are not tightly detailed; they are sketches of ideas for events and gatherings, leaving you room to adapt them. Throughout the chapter are contributions from other Forest Church groups to provide a wider perspective. The exercises need varying degrees of preparation; some you can simply go and do, others need more work but are well worth the effort. Don't let the more advanced activities put you off; they are here to show you the breadth of possible ideas and to inspire you with examples. But if all you can manage are short walks with some appropriate readings and poems, that is still Forest Church. For most of the more advanced activities, I've provided suggestions for simplified versions. And remember that it's a good idea for you to have tried the activity first before asking anyone else to do it. For walks, do the route the preceding week to check the paths.

JANUARY

LANDSCAPE READING

Landscape reading and the super senses workshop (described as the May example) form a solid foundation to nature connection. One is using the head to analyze an environment, and the other is using the senses to connect with a place and the processes of nature.

The low light and skeletal natural forms of January make this a good time for landscape reading, especially if there is frost or snow on the land—but you can do it any time of the year. On the downside, landscape reading is probably the one activity in this chapter that needs the most preparation or study; on the plus side, you may find that you know a lot of the elements already.

Landscape reading combines all sorts of disciplines (botany, geology, field ecology, history, etc.) and has all sorts of applications (planning, surveying, biodiversity monitoring), but perhaps the most important quality is that it's fun. It is all about observing the processes and relationships happening around you in nature and asking yourself what is going on. With a detective's eye, your gaze travels from the far horizon to what's at your feet, and as you piece the clues together, you can be amazed at the stories the land is telling you. It takes some preparation and Study, so this is a more advanced activity.

A typical landscape reading trip might last two to three hours and travel only half a mile or so, during which time you'll stop where there is something interesting to talk about. You might learn about the rock and soil under your feet and how to identify the trees you come across; you might look for signs of wild and domestic animals, and you might see evidence of human intervention, both contemporary and historical. The big stories any landscape reading trip will tell you fall into four categories:

Shaping Forces: These are the elements that result in the landscape you're looking at. These range from ancient forces to immediate, but they all interrelate; we're back to process again. The three main shaping forces are rock and soil, biotic (all living things, plants, animals and fungi—but, most important, humans), and climate and microclimate.

Succession: In most of the temperate land of the world, the environment is trying to *succeed* to mature forest; if it were left to its own devices, it would progress from soil to annuals to herbaceous scrub and perennials, and eventually to climax tree species. But when you look at most of the countryside, you're seeing the land held back from that process.

Biodiversity and Ecosystem Services: Different areas, whether they're natural, semi-natural, semi-improved, or improved, have a story to tell about biodiversity and sustainability. An alternative measure of value is the ecosystem services supplied by the environment. The latter may seem anthropocentric, but it is a relevant measure of an area's value.

The Sacred: Most of the United States has been occupied for more than 12,000 years, and succeeding waves of tribal and European peoples have formed their varied understandings of the landscape and sacred reality. Certain natural land-marks were "holy places" in their own right, tied to sacred observances or myths. An obvious sign of sacred landscape (assuming one knows where to look) is ancient rock art. In the Southwest, some paintings are still visible that were formed more than 5,000 years ago. Ancient Native peoples also left ruins—such as the imposing ritual mounds of the Hopewell people in the Midwest and earthworks that recall the vast cities of the Cahokia people in the South. If you look carefully at the placement of ruins and rock art, you can often gather a sense of how the natural landscape impressed the makers' minds to create holy sites that reflect their natural surroundings.

Secondary stories that could almost have their own categories are the history of the landscape and its use, mostly by humans, and natural navigation, which is just a lot of fun. There obviously isn't the space to do justice to the subject here, but it is included to encourage you to learn about it. There are links to further resources listed at the end of the book.

A simplified version of this activity would be to go out for a short walk with a mini-library of reference books on plants, animals, and insects and walk with the intention of moving quite slowly with time to stop and look things up in the books. Whenever you see something interesting in the landscape, try to work out what is going on.

FEBRUARY
(Imbolc is February 2nd)
SAINT BRIGID'S CROSS

(David Cole, facilitator of New Forest Forest Church [NFFC], has produced the following for February.)

INTRODUCTION

The natural beauty of the New Forest national park in England's Hampshire lends itself wonderfully to host a Forest Church branch. The 150 square miles of natural woodland and heathland, much of it "commoner" land, is famous for its New Forest ponies and different breeds of deer and donkey.

My own influence on NFFC has come from my studies of Christian mysticism and the ancient Celtic church. I belong to and work for a globally dispersed Celtic Christian Community, the Community of Aidan & Hilda. The spirituality of the Celts, the indigenous nations of the British Isles and Ireland long before the message of Christ came, was very deeply woven into the created order around them. When the message of Christ did come (within ten years of Jesus' death, according to Gildas the sixth-century historian, but well documented as being within one to two hundred years of Jesus' death, long before Augustine of Rome came), the idea of interweaving creation into their spirituality did not wane from the hearts and minds of the Celts.

The Celtic church believed that the Divine voice could be heard equally through the book of scripture and the book of Creation. When challenged as to how he could learn from God without access to any written scripture, a Celtic holy hermit took his accusers out of his hut, lifted his arms to the world around him, and said, "Here are my scriptures." The sixth-century Celtic monk Columbanus (who founded a monastery in Bobbio, where Francis of Assisi trained centuries later) taught his disciples that if they wanted to understand and get to know the Creator they must first understand and get to know Creation. These words are attributed to Ninian (who set up Christ-centered spiritual communities in what is now Scotland, years before Columba of Iona was born):

What is the fruit of study? To perceive the eternal Word of God reflected in every plant and insect, every bird and animal, every man and woman.

The Christian Celts knew and understood all that their ancestors knew and understood about the creation around them and the Divine presence which flowed through it.

In his book *The Book of Creation—The Practice of Celtic Spirituality,* J. Philip Newell states that "many of the holy sites and oak groves were transformed into monastic bases for Christian mission." This was not done in the same destructive way that the church of Rome did it, by knocking down the trees and stones, filling in the henges and building on top of them, but, as Newell continues, "Christ was preached as the fulfilment of everything that was true, including the wisdom of the tradition that preceded Christianity in Celtic Britain." In the same way, the early church preached that Jesus was the fulfilment of all that was true in the faith of the first-century Jews.

The inclusion of Creation in spirituality (or spirituality in Creation) was contrary to the teachings of the church of Rome, which taught the separation of things sacred and secular. From this dualistic perspective, the natural world did not need to be looked after. This was part of the great rift between the Celtic church and the church of Rome.

Today, many folk who are committed to walking in the ways of Christ are fed up with this separation and want to find a spiritual path that engages their love of Christ and their love and connectedness with creation. Modern expressions of the ancient Celtic Christian faith enable people to do this in an authentic Christ-focused way, and this is the foundation on which my focus for New Forest Forest Church is built.

Here at NFFC, we have had guided meditation walks using the physical things around us as metaphysical and metaphorical aspects of our spiritual journey, we've looked at the wisdom of the oak tree, and we've "considered the birds" (and other animals), as Jesus advised his disciples (Matt. 6:26). We have looked at the concept of being "led by quiet waters" (Ps. 23:2) and other sections of Psalms.

Within this activity, *italicized text* is to be spoken. The descriptive prose, not italicized, isn't intended to be read out verbatim; the ideas are there for you to absorb in preparation to be used more conversationally as you walk to somewhere sheltered to do the meditations and creative worship later in the activity.

REFLECTION ON SPRING

Spring is the first season of the Western year in which vegetation begins to appear. In the northern hemisphere, it is around March to May, and in the southern hemisphere around September to October. In Celtic tradition, "Imbolc" (the weeks between February 1 and April 30) is the spring season. Imbolc means something like "lamb's milk," which identifies this as the season of life.

Imbolc marks the end of winter and the return of the light; the end of the season of death and the beginning of the season of new birth. It is a time of beginnings, fresh inspiration, and planning for growth. It is a time to celebrate gestating life in the worlds of nature and the spirit. Spring is the time when we remember life returning after the "death" of winter, when new shoots and flowers begin to grow. It is a time of new things, and a time to remember rebirth and new life, as the trees start to bud and leaf again. Spring is a good time to rededicate your life to the Divine.

As you spend time walking among the plants and trees as they start to grow and bud and green again, look at them and contemplate your "new life" in Christ and your spiritual birth.

MEDITATION ON A SEED

Hold a seed in your hand. Run it through your fingers. Feel its smooth hard surface. Hold it up in your fingers and look at its contours. Look at how it is formed. The only purpose for this seed is to be planted and die, to be destroyed, and to allow the growth of the potential which it holds inside to come out and expand.

Imagine this seed is you, your inner self. Within you there is such great potential for growth and expansion, for life and beauty and creativity to be expressed, for your true self, the Divine image within you, to come out. But for this to happen, your false self, the ego, must "die."

Where and how do you need to be planted for this to happen?

SAINT BRIGID

February 1 is also the celebration of one of the leading Christian saints in the Celtic church who, through the years, through myth and legend, has become interwoven with an ancient Pagan goddess.

According to the *Annals of Ulster,* Brigid was born in Ireland in around 452 CE. She was born to a family who were possibly slaves to a Druid. Her mother was a Christian, converted by Patrick. It is possible that Brigid too heard Patrick speak when she was very young.

In Christian mythology, Brigid was known as the one who nurtured the "baby" faith that Patrick had planted; she became known as the midwife of the church in Ireland. The symbolic mythology of Brigid also grew into the idea that she was there at the birth of Christ and was the midwife to Mary and the baby Jesus themselves, perhaps a metaphysical explanation of her becoming known as the midwife of the church.

Brigid is also remembered as the embodiment of hospitality; she gave great feasts for the poor, she had deep compassion for those in need, and she often gave things away.

She also taught the benefit of having what the Celts called an *anamchara*, a "soul friend," a spiritual mentor and companion on life's path. A quote attributed to Brigid is "a person without a soul friend is like a body without a head."

She ran a mixed-gender community of God in Kildare, which became one of the largest and longest-running communities of God in Ireland.

Brigid's life is remembered on February 1, the date she died in 523 CE, which is also the first day of Imbolc, when Brigid, the life-giving goddess of the Pagans, traveled around the Earth, spreading her magic of new life. You can see why the two Brigids became interwoven!

The Christian Brigid was known to have traveled around sharing the gospel by the way she lived, in a way similar to our modern-day Mother Teresa. One day, so the legend goes, Brigid came upon a wounded Druid at the side of the road by a river. They spoke for some time as Brigid began to tend his wounds with the herbal knowledge she had. The Druid asked her about her faith and this "Jesus" of whom she spoke. Legend says that to help explain the story of Jesus, Brigid made a cross out of the reeds from the riverbank. Today, many Christians remake a "Brigid Cross" on this day to remind them of Brigid's life and message.

Find some reeds, straw, or paper straws and, following the instructions on the next page, create a "Brigid's Cross."

While you make the cross, you can contemplate the following:

How has my faith been nurtured?
Who has been a part of that? (Thank God for them.)
To whom have I shown compassion recently?
With whom have I shared my faith recently, by the way I live and the words I speak?
With whom do I share my life's path?
Who is my anamchara?

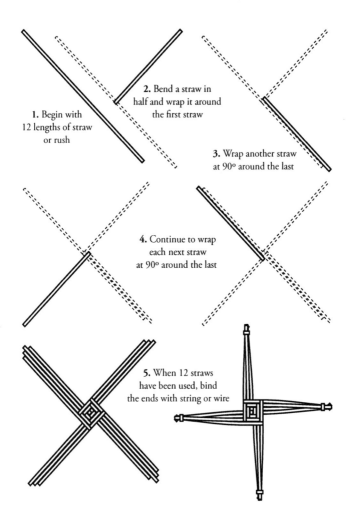

1. Begin with 12 lengths of straw or rush

2. Bend a straw in half and wrap it around the first straw

3. Wrap another straw at 90° around the last

4. Continue to wrap each next straw at 90° around the last

5. When 12 straws have been used, bind the ends with string or wire

LIGHT

Imbolc is also the season to celebrate the returning of the light. In the Christian calendar, February 2 is *Candlemas,* the Christian festival of light. It is traditionally remembered as the day on which Jesus was presented at the Temple, and Simeon called him the "light to the Gentiles." In pre-Christian days it was the *Feast of Lights,* being the day halfway between the Winter Solstice and the Spring Equinox.

Light enables us to see. The more light, the more clearly you can see. Light can also be an inner work of spiritual discipline. The mystics call this *Fotosis* or *Illuminativia.* The application of this is inner cleansing: time spent cleaning the windows of your soul from the grime of life and negativity to enable more light to come in. Light dispels darkness; with light there can be no darkness.

Why not spend some time, as Spring unfolds, practicing the ancient spiritual discipline of Illuminativia?

Scripture Reflection

Jesus said: "I am the Light of the world. Whoever follows me will never walk in darkness, but will have the light of life" (John 8:12).
What does this mean to you?
Jesus also said: "You are the light of the world, a city on a hill cannot be hidden . . . let your light shine before others" (Matt. 5:14–16).
What does this mean to you?

Closing Benediction

May you know the potential which has been placed within you. May you be a positive expression of the Divine image within you. May you allow the Divine Light to shine into your soul. And may you be one who shines out that same light into the world, dispelling darkness and negativity and bringing light and life.

March
(the Spring Equinox is March 21st)
Growing Food

The Spring Equinox marks the beginning of the lighter half of the year. The land still holds the cold but it is possible to start some kind of food growing with the idea of sharing the harvest later on in the year as part of a feast and celebration, perhaps in August or September. This is a way to get involved in the rhythms of the natural world and recognize our dependence on nature for our survival. This activity also encourages us to eat local, fresh food, while keeping fit doing the work. You will also have a reason to get out and connect with nature as you tend your crops.

In essence, the idea is to gather together in someone's garden, allotment, or community space and work together to sow early potatoes, onions, shallots, and garlic, rows of peas and seeds of all kinds, and some salad crops (some of this will need to be under cover). There may be other jobs to do, like building raised beds or preparing the ground for growing. Later in the year you might gather together to harvest the food during a celebration or shared meal of some kind. If you or anyone else in your group has horticultural experience, you might like to be responsible for preparation and facilitation. Having done this a number of times with different groups, I can tell you it is simple, rewarding, and socially bonding

An extension of the idea is to share responsibility for various crops among the group. Different plants could be sown in modules or trays, and each participant who has some garden space could take them away to look after them for the growing period.

You may also like to introduce a moment of prayer or ceremony to draw links between the activity and God's Spirit in nature. You might like to go further and do a Spring Equinox ritual during the gathering.

April
WALK WITH REFLECTIONS

In every walk with Nature
one receives far more than he seeks.
John Muir

This is a simple, accessible, and enjoyable activity that can be used regularly. In Mid Wales, we do this four times a year. The idea is to walk as a group and stop a few times to listen to a site-specific reading, poem, or meditation.

To prepare this, you need to have a route in mind that has on it a few useful features such as bridges, lakes, hilltops, or gorges, and put together some kind of theme that connects the features with the material you want to read. This way, people end up making both an external and internal journey. Good readings can come from just about anywhere: poetry books, sacred text, Internet collections, and your own writing.

A good way to start is to ask the members of the group to walk in silence for three periods, perhaps five minutes each, where they focus first on just what they can see (using owl or hawk eyes, see May), then to focus on what they can hear, and last, to focus on what they can feel (their feet falling on the path, their balance, the feel of their clothes on their body as they move, the play of air on exposed skin).

A similar suggestion, perhaps for later in a walk, is to ask the group to walk in silence and solitude with about 50 feet between each person. If someone stops to make a note or to look at something, then everyone else has to stop too.

May
(Beltane is May 1st)
AWAKENING SUPER SENSES

This Super Senses workshop is a great preparation for Awe, as a way into reading the Second Book of God. In other words, if you're wanting to connect with nature mindfully, doing so with your senses is a good start. It is also an opportunity to have fun.

We connect to nature through our senses, and some researchers suspect there may be more of these than the five we think we've got. Our embodied senses form a foundation, but we also have some Super Senses that we've forgotten how to use. If you can find some examples of people using Supers Senses, those stories can make a good introduction to the workshop.

ACTIVITIES TO SHARPEN THE SENSES

Counting Sounds: This is a good way to begin many gatherings in nature. I often use this exercise to get people to focus on the present place and moment. Ask your participants to close their eyes and hold both their hands out with their fists closed. Ask them to count, by opening their fingers one by one, each new sound they hear from a different source.

Fifteen Example Senses: Allow your participants time to contribute ideas and examples of various senses, going beyond the five we think of first.

- sight, hearing, touch, taste, smell
- proprioception (see the next page)
- direction
- balance
- time
- appetite and hunger
- temperature and temperature change
- sense of season
- sensing humidity
- sense of pressure, in water and from sound
- awareness of one's own visibility

Michael J. Cohen, one of the founders of ecopsychology, explores a list of over fifty senses in his book *Reconnecting sith Nature.*

Floating Like a Leaf: This is a lovely way to explore proprioception (which is the sense of knowing where you, or your limbs, are in space), if you have some willing participants.

One person lies on the ground with his eyes closed and his hands crossed over his chest; he is the leaf. Somewhere between six and eight other participants carefully lift him in this horizontal position to a comfortable height, the average chest height of the lifters. I make sure there is someone responsible at the head end, and I'll warn those prepared to be the leaf that there will be lots of hands reaching under them to lift them up (most people find this quite pleasant).

The lifters as a group, in silence, carry the horizontal person in a figure eight or a loop to turn him around in space, ending up where they started. When they get back to roughly the starting position, they begin to gently sway the person/leaf backward and forward as they slowly lower him back to the ground, like a leaf floating down through the air.

Ask the person/leaf how his experience was and whether he knew where he was in space. Then give someone else a turn.

The first time you do this you may want to break the silence to run through the exercise and give your participants an idea of the techniques necessary to lift someone up. If you have a big gathering, you can split into groups of around eight.

ANIMAL FORMS

These provide a way to explore our senses within the framework of a game, which gives us license to play. The following six exercises run together quite nicely. Remember the overarching reason behind these activities is to give your participants tools to enable them to connect with nature, not just for this gathering but at other times too.

Owl Eyes: Stand relaxed, looking in front of you. Let your focus soften and move your attention to your peripheral vision. A good way to explore the extent of your peripheral vision is with wiggly fingers. Hold your arms straight in front of you and wiggle your fingers, then move your hands out to either side as far as they'll go until you can just barely see your fingers wiggling. You can do the same above and below, tracing the edge of your sphere of vision. Let your arms relax but maintain the Owl Eyes awareness. What movements can you see at the edges? What colors and differences in tone can you detect?

Hawk Eyes: By contrast, Hawk Eyes gets you to look through the pinpoint focus of a hawk, giving all your attention to the tiniest spot. With practice it is possible to combine the two ways of looking.

Deer Ears: Our eyes tend to become our dominant sense, but our ears have the potential to sense much farther and from behind as well as in front. Prey animals, such as deer and rabbits, extend their awareness far beyond what they can see, partly by hearing danger directly but also by listening to the distant call of birds responding to predators (this is called bird language).

Stand facing toward a distant sound such as a stream. Cup your hands behind your ears to mimic the shape of a deer's ears; you should be able to hear more clearly and with more focus. Next, turn 180 degrees with your back toward the sound source. This time cup your hands in front of your ears to magnify sounds behind you. Using these two techniques, possibly with your eyes closed, listen to all the sounds around you, in front and behind. Are the sounds constant or fluctuating or sudden? What is the closest sound you can hear, and what is the farthest away?

Raccoon Touch: Raccoons have sensitive and dextrous "hands" that they use to search for food. The focus of this game is on our sense of touch. You'll need a supply of similarly sized stones, pebbles, or sticks. Each participant chooses five or six stones (or sticks) that are as similar as possible. With your eyes closed, select one of the stones and feel its every surface until you think you could identify it from the others. Open your eyes and make sure you could identify the stone from the others by sight (you may need to mark it with a pen). Place the stone with the others. With your eyes closed again, the task is to find your stone using just touch.

There are lots of other touch-based games, often using blindfolds. One, for example, has people working in pairs, where one is blindfolded and led by the other on a touch-based exploration of an environment. A variation on the stone game, using this pairing, is for the blindfolded player to be led to a tree to touch, in order to identify it from five or so other trees.

Fox Walking: When we move through woodland or any rough terrain, with the intention of connecting with nature, or to follow bird language or track animals, it's essential to walk silently, the way a fox or stalking cat walks. The easiest way to learn this is to experiment with different techniques and compare notes. You can play a related game, Grandmother's Footsteps, to put this to the test. Site yourselves where the ground cover will provide some challenges and have someone stand in the center with her eyes closed or blindfolded. Everyone else forms a circle a good distance away around the central player, and the winner is the one who can touch the middle player (or pick up a set of keys from just in front of her, if you want a greater challenge) without being detected. If the central player hears anything, she points in that direction, so if a player gets pointed at, he has to return to his starting point.

Dog Nose: To put your sense of smell to the test, you can attempt to follow a scent trail. Without anyone else watching, make a short trail using some natural scents such as essential oils mixed with water in a sprayer or an air freshener that only uses 100 percent natural ingredients. Then see if your participants can follow the trail. If you're somewhere open on an even surface, try doing this blindfolded. Encourage your participants to try different techniques to follow the trail. Scanning left and right with many short sniffs seems to work the best.

Body Radar: Now it is time to build on the previous awareness games and introduce a deeper sense of discernment or sensitivity to the soul of a place, its *anima loci.* The idea of body radar is to move with no conscious agenda, to go where your soul leads you. This is best played individually and somewhere where there are many directions of travel possible—an open stretch of forest, for example. Stand and turn slowly to feel or discern which is the right way to go; perhaps even ask which direction you are being called toward. Some people try to sense this by holding their hands in front of them. Continue to move slowly, and whenever you're faced with a split in the path, ask yourself the same questions. Use the exercise to find somewhere to go and be still for fifteen minutes or so. Then return to the starting place.

Many people often feel what they might describe as energy in different places. Recently, I took a group on a landscape-reading workshop and stopped outside an unassuming garage down a side street. I happened to know that hidden at the back of the garage was the healing well on which the original Celtic settlement was founded. With no preamble, I asked if anyone in the group could sense anything. A few people could; someone even said she thought there might have been a healing well there.

The body radar exercise above can be used without an agenda, but it can also be used with an agenda or a question, perhaps to find something or to be led to something of meaning. Many people will make links between the idea of using body radar with an agenda and the concept of dowsing.

Silent Stalker: This fascinating game is a further development of the sense games already explored. The mechanics are that the participants stand in a circle around a central player who chooses to be a prey animal of some kind, such as a rabbit, deer, or mouse. The person, or the group, then decides on an archetypal predator for that prey animal, such as a fox, wolf, or cat. Once the central player is blindfolded, someone is nominated silently by the facilitator to be the predator animal. She has to stand and point with both arms out straight toward the prey, embodying everything that the hungry animal would be thinking about the prey, staring at him with total concentration and intensity. Everyone else in the group must be passive, dropping their heads to look at the ground between them and the prey, holding their arms by their sides, becoming like trees. (They can watch what happens with owl eyes.) The player in the middle, the prey, then has to turn slowly and point in the direction he feels the threat is coming from.

You could give players two or three tries, and if you have children playing, you might want to say warm or cold, but you might be surprised by how often you don't need to give someone a second guess. Quite often, and I'm not sure why, the prey will point in the opposite direction with his first guess. With this sort of game, I explain the rules and ask for volunteers to take the middle prey position. The silent stalker game is a great prompt for conversation. You can begin the game by asking if anyone has ever had the experience of feeling like she were being watched.

JUNE
(the Summer Solstice is June 21st)
TEA CEREMONY

The idea of a tea ceremony came from time spent foraging, recognizing that the plants we were collecting were unique expressions of the Christ-created world around us. When you see a burdock leaf (which is edible) as something that the Divine Spirit made and sustains, what does it mean to pick it and eat it?

Many plants are edible, and many make delicious tea, and those plants can also carry deep meaning. The following is an example of a tea ceremony, exploring a theme using four different ingredients carefully picked and dried in advance, but if you have some foraging and plant-lore expertise, you can adapt the idea quite easily to use different ingredients. Remember that the Meaning of plants can be discerned through direct, primary study, not just from traditional or contemporary plant-lore sources, which may derive their ideas from customs and superstitions no longer relevant in our time.

(Within the following activity, *italicized text* is to be spoken.)

Begin in a circle. Draw two lines forming a cross in line with the compass. These lines represent the four cardinal directions, east and west, north and south. Take some time to turn in each of these directions, wander away if necessary, and use your senses to attune to this place. Slowly go through each sense in turn, seeing, hearing, smelling for each direction. (You could share the following among different readers.)

God of the East, the sun rising and the fruitful earth.
We call to you, to bring us light.

God of the West, sun setting, and the ocean.
We call to you, to bring us peace.

God of the North and the mountains.
We call to you, to give us your perspective.

God of the South and the warm breeze.
We call to you, to be the embrace between us.

Draw a circle to enclose the four directions, like a Celtic cross. As the circle is drawn, say:

The circle of our ceremony,
the circle of our seasons,
the circle of our lives,
and the circle of God around us.

Welcome to this circle and a Tea Ceremony of this place and for this time. The theme and blessing of this ceremony is regeneration.

Discover in yourself the expectancy and longing to connect with something bigger than yourself.

Pause for reflection.

The deep peace of the Great Spirit, be with us.
The bright openness of this vast sky, illuminate us.
The silent praise of the hills and trees, inspire us.
The rich mystery of the fertile soil, regenerate us.
God, whose love excludes no one, be with us.

TEA MAKING

We use a large glass jug or teapot to make the tea, and if possible, have a fire or camp stove to boil the water. The ingredients can be picked and dried in advance: mullein leaves, hawthorn flowers and leaves, elderflowers, and birch leaves. These trees and plants are all common across North America, growing along roadsides, on farmland, and even, on occasion, in empty city lots.

The tea we're about to make will contain four ingredients that grow in this place. These four plants all represent regeneration in different ways. So this tea and this ceremony is a blessing for regeneration, in your life and how you impact the world.

As we describe the nature of these plants, think about regeneration needs in your life or in the life of your community and see what resonates with you. See what you would like a blessing for.

MULLEIN

The first ingredient is mullein, which is traditionally drunk to relieve the symptoms of coughs, bronchitis, and sore throats. It represents courage, protection, exorcism, health, and regeneration of our bodies.

Think of mullein if you need an inner sense of affirmation and protection. And think of mullein if you need to be brave and grasp something initially difficult.

HAWTHORN

Hawthorn is a tea traditionally drunk as a heart and circulation tonic, blended from leaves and flowers plucked in the spring and haws picked in the autumn.

It represents regeneration through the hardness of its wood, its resilience to the elements and its affinity with the heart.

Think of the energy of hawthorn when what needs regenerating needs a strong heart. And as Christ's crown, think of hawthorn when sacrifice is needed.

ELDERFLOWER

Elderflower was once known as the medicine chest of the common people. It is traditionally drunk as a tea with antiviral effects during fevers and for chest complaints.

This most bountiful of trees represents regeneration through its associations with voice, song, and music.

If your regeneration needs a clear plan and a strong voice, think of what elder represents. And remember that a single flower is insignificant but makes a powerful blend in community.

BIRCH

The four teas move from body to heart to voice to soul. The final ingredient is the pioneer birch. Tasting similar to green tea, it has traditionally been drunk as a spring tonic.

It represents regeneration through its abundance and its role in the process of succession of forming soil and habitat.

Think of birch if you're starting something on new territory. And remember its meaning when you need to get the groundwork sorted first.

BREWING

While the tea is brewing, I invite you to name out loud something that you're regenerating. Something that you would welcome a blessing for. For the rest of us, can we hold what we hear in our thoughts?

SHARING

The tea is poured into two glass cups to be shared. Each person takes a sip and passes the cup to the next person. If the tea is still very hot, you can add some cold water.

As we share the tea we say:
Every blessing of the Great Spirit be with you.

FINAL BLESSING

Great Spirit, and source of all, as this summer revives and restores us, may you nurture our dreams, enliven our energy, and regenerate our spirits. In the name of Christ.

JULY
LABYRINTH

With any luck the weather in July should be good for creating a labyrinth for participants to walk. This is a contemplative activity that can create moments of Awe for people. Labyrinths, unlike mazes, aren't designed to get you lost, but to guide you on a journey inward and then outward, a journey that mirrors pilgrimage and even life as a whole.

You can create labyrinths in lots of different ways, from lines drawn in sand on a beach to paths mown in grass. You could mark them out with ribbon or stones or with paper bags part-filled with sand holding nightlights. A quick search online can show you various patterns, including the classic one at Chartres Cathedral. My favorite is the Ely Cathedral labyrinth, partly because it can be laid out to emphasize the four cardinal directions, but also because the first route into it, almost but not quite, takes you to the center; lots of meaning can be found in that. Both of these are quite a challenge to recreate on the ground, but the Cretan labyrinth diagrammed on this page is straightforward.

You can create the labyrinth and let people find their own meaning while walking it, but some people find that a bit of a challenge, so you could provide them with some content to help them—either before they begin or during the journey. These could be in the form of short readings or short, ritualistic activities.

August
(Lughnasadh is August 1st)
INVOLVING CHILDREN

(Matt Freer, involved in Forest Church in the Oxford area in the UK, has contributed these thoughts.)

If I'd been by myself I would have completely missed it, but as it was, my four-year-old daughter saw it. She had just been on my back as we went on a "midnight" walk through a little wood. Now, with a heightened sense of bravery after admiring a bat flitting about under an oak tree, she had asked to get down to walk on her own. It was then that she spotted the lizard on the soil at the edge of the field where we were walking. As we watched the lizard, she marveled at how good it would be at playing Red Light/Green Light. I marveled at how attentive and open she was to the creatures around us hidden in the twilight.

I tell this story because it highlights what so many of us know: we adults often miss precious things our children don't. This fact is highlighted very obviously by Jesus in the Gospels, and yet the gifts children offer the church are often missed. We shoehorn children's activities into the rest of "church," and we make sure these activities fit with our adult objectives of keeping children quiet while we get on with "real" church.

The concept of Forest Church tips this worn approach on its head. The Forest School movement in the UK puts children at the center of their learning—and I am excited that as expressions of Forest Church develop, new ways of putting children at the center of church will emerge.

The concept of "Forest Church" comes naturally to children, and they are in many ways going to be the teachers to us adults as far as nature connection goes. This in part requires us adults to approach things openly and perhaps differently from the ways in which we are accustomed to do things. We need to enable children to be our teachers, and then ensure that we as adults have eyes to see and ears to hear what they teach us.

One of the many things children can help us with is slowing down. Children quite naturally focus on the details, the little moments. This "slow gift" often forces us adults to slow down as well, which can open up our approach to nature. It also changes how much distance we can cover in, say, a Forest Church walk, which can be frustrating. We need to learn to embrace it, and plan our activities so that everyone can enjoy them. It is a balancing act. We don't want to miss what children offer.

Here are some key principles for nurturing a child's spirituality.

Authenticity: Connecting children with nature requires adults who are connected too. Children recognize hypocrisy. It is no good espousing the benefits of connecting with nature if we adults don't share the same sense of connection with nature. You've got to actively join in!

Encouragement: How much do we listen to the experiences and reflections our children have with nature? Always seek to affirm your children's imagination and sense of wonder. Make time. Ask questions that draw their attention to nature.

Rituals and rhythms: What rituals and rhythms can we introduce into our daily life and home that connect with nature? A few ideas: lighting candles, blessing food, nature tables, special places in the back yard, and favorite walks.

The gentle art of listening: We need to listen to our child's reflections as fully as possible, but avoid artificial "Let's sit and talk now" situations. Instead, create opportunities to share at home and outdoors (for example, simply going for a walk together, away from intrusive distractions).

Special activities: The day-to-day activities are important, but so are the special occasions like a "midnight walk." These need to be planned and made special.

A Forest Church activity might be a walk in the dark, which is great for heightening the senses, but these activities need to be planned to open the senses, not to scare. It will depend on the children involved. For example, if you have a lot of toddlers around the age of two in your group, you may want to go out slightly earlier than if you have children four and upward, but if each child is with a parent you should be fine. The facilitator should know the route well and have a good idea of where to stop to see and hear certain creatures—although as I have pointed out above, it is the children who will usually see the things we don't, so the facilitator's job is more about creating the right opportunities. A good tip is to use red light from torches or bike lights, since it doesn't interfere with night vision the way white light does. (It takes about twenty minutes to fully adjust to darkness.) If you do the same walk in the daylight, children can contrast the differences between day and night.

A few Awe-inspiring variations on this activity are worth investigating. These are the kinds of things that create special memories that last a lifetime. Some of these might mean more to older children. Here are three examples:

Lightning bugs: If you're anywhere near undeveloped grassland, you may spot lightning bugs in the hours after dusk between late May and early September, peaking in mid-July. They thrive near rotting wood and moist earth.

A starling murmuration: Children will enjoy the spectacular aerial display put on by end-of-summer flocks of starlings as they gather at dusk just before settling to roost. You'll need to find out your local starling roosts. They like urban areas, such as railway stations and powerlines, but they also like reedy marshes and open fields.

Meteor showers: If you're lucky enough to live somewhere with low light pollution, and even more lucky to have a cloudless night—and you're game enough to get up in the small hours of the night—then consider a gathering to watch one of the more predictable meteor showers. Search for the current year's Perseids, Leonids, and Geminids, for example. You'll need to wrap up warmly for this adventure.

September
(the Autumn Equinox is September 21st)
Inventing a Group Ritual

Rituals are often based on traditional patterns. The strength of this approach is the legacy of the tradition, the ease with which those familiar with the pattern can enter a deeper state, the sense of connection between participants—and the ready-made structure it provides the leader, saving time on creating content. But there is a danger that a ritual's meaning and impact gets lost in the repetition, and its freshness and relevance no longer connect with our changing times.

Facilitated groups can create their own rituals as events in themselves. This can be done with seriousness and solemnity—or it can be a fun, creative game. Either way, this is an activity that can be especially bonding, creating a moment of deep meaning and relevance to the participants, since they will all have contributed to it. It is a good activity at the interplay of Awe and Meaning.

At the appropriate moment, in the appropriate way, introduce the exercise to the group and let creativity fly. You may need to facilitate here and there to keep the process moving. It is really as simple as that. If you instinctively feel that you understand this idea, you probably don't need any further direction.

The first time I facilitated this exercise, I'd been co-coaching a group of executives on an intensive seven-day wilderness trip in the Picos Mountains in Spain. We were on our sixth day, and we had spent the morning canoeing down a river. We were finishing a lazy lunch on a sandbank, and it felt like an appropriate moment to try this. I remember being nervous about how it would be received—but I needn't have been. The element that most stands out in my mind is the sculpture that was created out of natural materials as a centerpiece.

With many groups, there are moments when the energy is right, that call out to be marked somehow, as if a ritual is needed to provide a depth of expression—a way of allowing participants to say something individually, while collectively forming or strengthening a deeper bond.

It may be that the ritual is never repeated, or it may become the beginning of something that gets developed over time. Depending on your situation, you can introduce the exercise with no direction at all, or you could provide some ingredients or parameters if that helps get things going. If you don't plan to use this exercise as the main focus of a gathering, keep it up your sleeve to introduce more informally when the moment is right.

It is a good addition to a combination of related exercises you could use to choose somewhere as a sacred meeting place or grove. You could combine this exercise with a group Body Radar (from May) and wandering (chapter 4) exercise, the goal being to discern a sacred space in a natural area and undertake some kind of ceremony there in participation with the location's *anima loci*.

OCTOBER
WRITING A PSALM

At the heart of this activity is an exercise in Meaning-making. Writing a psalm is a creative exercise that encourages you to begin to explore and describe the dynamics of the nature-human-Divine connection.

Of course, many of the psalms from the Bible are full of natural references and provide good inspiration. You don't need a license or a qualification, by the way; anyone is allowed to write a psalm! Having said that, some people are nervous about sharing their work with others, so make it clear that no one will be made to share.

A good way to structure this event is to place it within a walk or wander somewhere inspirational and dramatic, if you have that option on your doorstep. You could use the walking time to encourage discussion around the themes and meaning people are able to draw or discern from the environment.

You might want to provide a postcard-sized sheet of notes to help. Having access to the Bible's psalms would help; you could read aloud examples to help your participants understand the structure. When you're ready to write, the exercise could more or less follow this structure:

1.   Spend some time in contemplation to determine a theme inspired by your location and what you want to say about God.

2. Make the language personal, experiential, sensual, and descriptive.
3. In your psalm, recognize God's generosity or list your blessings. Describe how you're able to be thankful.
4. Worship, affirming God's goodness.
5. Try writing in parallel pairs (or more) of lines as the psalmists often did (provide examples of these). There are three versions of this. The first uses pairs of lines that say the same thing differently: the second line echoes the idea in the first (the technical term for this is synonymous parallelism, but that's not essential to know). The second version of parallel thoughts does the opposite: the second line reverses or opposes the first, often with the word "but" (this is called antithetic parallelism). The third version, synthetic parallelism, has the second line develop the sentiment in the first.

Here are two examples of contemporary psalms. The first is inspired by the Dales countryside in the UK, and the second I wrote after a trip foraging for mushrooms.

Psalm of the Dales
by Fran Langridge

Blessed art Thou, Lord of the Universe.
All creation declares Your glory.
Blessed art Thou who created the hills,
Who planted the bilberries and the heather.
Blessed art Thou who spread the sky,
Who painted the clouds and the rainbow.
The sunshine proclaims Your warming love;
The thunder and the downpour Your mighty power.
By the unending cycle of the waters
Do You sustain creation's life.

You cleanse the Earth in winter;
Faithfully You grant awaited spring.
The snowdrop and the lamb show Your tenderness
All mankind responds to Your beauty.
Almighty God of greenness and birdsong,
We praise You.

Mushroom Hunter's Psalm

The Lord is my delight: when I expect autumn,
he brings harvest.
The Lord is my provision: when I am dwarfed
by my landscape, he makes me live.
The wise seek and taste the Lord's blessings,
but the ignorant taste nothing.
You fill my basket with the choicest fruits.
You fill my soul with creation's mystical song.
In the dark, I am blind to the ways you feed my life.
Me, myself, isolated, I don't see the fruits beyond my reach.
My roots stand in contaminated soil.
Give me wisdom to know good from bad,
to choose life over death, and to speak your
praise as you ever feed my soul.

A simplified (but creatively limited) version is to write a psalm by answering a series of questions, each of which results in a line of the psalm.

1. Think of a way to address God and say how God is like something from nature around you *(e.g., Divine Creator, your love flows like the rushing river).*
2. Find another way to say what you said in the first line *(like a refreshing spring, your love is constant).*
3. What, inspired by nature, can you thank God for? *(I thank you for the bright sunshine. . .)*

4. Why are you thankful for that?
5. What else can you thank God for?
6. What difference does the thing for which you are thankful make to the world?
7. Write a line about something big and possibly scary that you've noticed in nature.
8. How does that make you feel?
9. How would you hope God would help you?
10. What good things would you hope God would remind you of from your trip into nature?

NOVEMBER

(Samhain is on the 1st)

ADVENT WREATH

(Matt Arnold, facilitator of East Midlands Forest Church [EMFC] has produced the following for November.)

INTRODUCTION

When we set up EMFC, we were responding to a call to take church to where people were. People attending our local Mind, Body, Spirit fair had a negative view of religion, while regarding themselves as spiritual; Christians, in their eyes, were not very spiritual people and had often caused hurt. People weren't interested in an intellectual presentation of Christianity; they wanted experiences, not head knowledge.

In 2012, several threads joined: an interest in the natural world, the New Spiritualities movements, and Christian multisensory worship and meditation. When Mid Wales Forest Church started, I saw an opportunity to combine these and take church into the place where I felt called, outdoors into the natural created order. East Midlands Forest Church was born.

Initially, we saw Forest Church as a time of going out into nature, doing Bible readings, thoughts, and meditation, all based around the Celtic Wheel of the Year. We now weave into these rituals, liturgy, chanting, kinesthetic activities, drum work, and times of sharing our thoughts during the gathering.

We do try to include activities that help people to engage with the Eternal Spirit between group meetings, as well as encouraging people to use their talents where possible in the production of materials for the group. Our *style* could be classed as *Pagan,* but the *content* is *Christian,* something that has taken me out of my comfort zone into uncharted waters. We do have prayer partners and people within the Christ Tradition who review our materials, and we have the backing of our local church. We are all on a journey together toward somewhere none of us have been before, toward the Divine Creator. Christ is our compass; we simply follow where he leads us.

ADVENT WREATH ACTIVITY

The goal of this activity is for each participant or family to build an Advent wreath that can be used in the days before Christmas, perhaps just as a table decoration or as the center of a month's worth of ritual and reflection. If you haven't got enough materials on hand for everyone to build a wreath, you could use the event to go for a walk to collect materials to make one as a demonstration. You can share the symbolism of the plants used in the wreath, either on the walk or when you're making the wreaths.

The simple wreath just sits round a central candle, but the ritual wreath has another four colored candles at the cardinal points. For instructions and liturgy for each of the Sundays leading to Advent, see forestchurch.co.uk.

If you make the wreath with the materials listed below, it should be fully compostable. Alternatively you can make the wreath around a wire-and-moss ring.

You will need:

- Six or seven willow withes or something similar (dogwood, hazel, broom, etc.) to form the basic ring.
- Natural fiber, string, or cordage that you've made.
- One platter or tray big enough to hold the ring with a couple of inches on either side.
- One white candle and holder that fits within the center of the wreath. (People may have their own candles and holders at home.)
- Evergreen (fir, hemlock, spruce, pine), ivy, and/or holly branches collected previously or as part of the activity. (Use gardening gloves to protect your hands—about three small branches of each plant should be enough for each wreath.)
- One each of red, green, yellow, and blue candles if you're wanting to do the ritual wreath.

Begin making the willow ring using the withes (and string if you need it). If you're making this for the ritual wreath, it needs to be strong enough to hold the four candles upright.

Once the basic ring is finished, make the wreath using the greenery you've collected, weaving the stems into the willow ring. Start with evergreen branches around the edges and then the holly and ivy on top. Fill any gaps with small evergreen branches.

For the ritual wreath, place the green candle securely between the withes at the north position; the blue goes at the south, the red goes west, and the yellow east. Place the candle holder into the center, and put the white candle into it.

Evergreen is an ancient symbol of eternal life, or survival after death, which explains why it is often found in graveyards. The evergreen can symbolize survival. While the earth is at rest, the evergreen stands tall and proud against all that the winter season throws at it. It is a joyful sight to behold: after the crunch of feet on freshly laid snow, you see its silhouette dusted with sparkling white ice crystals. Pine resin itself is a refreshing fragrance and lifts our spirits when burned as an incense.

Holly symbolizes the wintry realms, the darker half of the year. It stands for dignity and serenity, even in the face of great challenge, and it also symbolizes protection. It is while we are protected that we may experience peace in dark or trying times. Will this season be a time of peace for us, amid our consumerist culture?

Ivy symbolizes connection and friendship: the twists and turns our relationships take as we continue to grow and interweave. During this coming season, we are encouraged in our tradition to give gifts to each other to honor these connections and show our love and appreciation for the relationships we share. Our consumerist culture attempts to link the amount of love with the expense of the gift, a trap many fall into. How will we be able to show love and connectedness with the human and non-human world around us?

December
(the Winter Solstice is on the 21st)
WINTER SOLSTICE RITUAL

(This introduction and activity were written by Alison Eve of Ancient Arden Forest Church in the West Midlands in the UK.)

INTRODUCTION

The Ancient Arden Forest Church, based in the Midlands, held its first ritual at the Autumn Equinox in 2012. Our concern is to explore relationships with the natural world, surf the boundaries between Christianity and Paganism, and discover God in her Goddess aspect. We seek to be non-judgmental, offering a place where no one is made to feel inadequate because of individual beliefs and practices, while hosting the broadest possible navigation of the Christian tradition.

WINTER SOLSTICE

While using the motif of the birth of light into the world as an icon of our own Christ-natures, our own inner lights, this Winter Solstice ritual incorporates Pagan aspects such as the burning of the Yule Log. Although Trinitarian in expression, the basic structure will be familiar to Pagans, since it involves all the usual elements of a Druidic ritual. We have adapted this within a monotheistic framework, but that framework is by no means rigid and the language leaves space for those of different traditions to enter into the ritual in a meaningful way.

Both here and at our Samhain ritual, we take care not to replicate the usual Christian polarity of light and dark as good and evil, but to learn from our Pagan friends: dark is a place of learning and growth, not something to be rejected or prayed against. This involves consideration of the Dark Mother, sometimes regarded by Pagans as the Goddess in her Crone aspect. The lessons she has to impart are difficult ones and must be respected as such. The ritual leaders should be aware of the possible repercussions for themselves as they prepare to contain the energy of the group. Be prepared for disturbed nights and surprising lessons.

I have been very specific in the fauna and flora honored during our ritual, so you will need to adapt this to suit your setting, but the cedar tree is a good starting point. Look for that significant element of the landscape, the feature that defines and shapes the space around it, and you will begin to experience a closer relationship with the *anima loci*, the spirit of place. This is what sets Forest Church apart from other outdoors church activities: we are putting ourselves in a place where we may begin to have a relationship with the non-human world. We may encounter and experience things that we cannot fit into our usual Christian theories—and we'll be the richer for it.

At the start of the ritual, the leader needs to set up the intention, as in the opening paragraph below, and then continue holding this on behalf of the group as the space is prepared and the circle woven. Weaving a circle is one of the most basic aspects of this type of ritual and seeks to create a temporary sacred space where we can meet in peace. Before the ritual, it is a good idea to talk about the sacred circle, what it might mean for us, and how we can help by, for example, visualizing a surrounding circle of light. Several of the opening elements of the ritual structure have been combined into a song: weaving the circle, calling for peace, and honoring the three worlds of earth, sea, and sky.

The calling of the Four Quarters is another key component, and we have used many models for this, such as Saint Francis's Brother Sun and Sister Moon at Samhain. We invite the inherent qualities associated with north, south, east, and west to assist in our ritual. You will find many different associations as you work with circles and rituals.

The ritual year can be said to begin at different locations on the Wheel of the Year. In our branch of Forest Church, we decided to end one year at Samhain and start the next at the Winter Solstice, with the long dark season of waiting and watching in between. The ritual action of the Winter Solstice is then a natural continuation from the work we began at Samhain, acknowledging the blessings of the dark. Our challenge is to make this time between Samhain and the Solstice as quiet as possible in our personal lives—not easy with Christmas and all its activities.

For the Yule Log, you need a large, whole piece of wood, decorated with naturally flammable materials such as evergreens, natural-fiber ribbons, etc. The remains of this year's log will be used to kindle next year's Yule Fire as a symbol of hope and prosperity for the year ahead.

With the fire lit, it is a good time for storytelling, and in this ritual we offer a Hebridean folk legend told to me by Sister Fionn of the Ceile De.

When you pass out the food, you might like to offer the first portion to the wildlife who will move in when you have gone. We do this following Pagan tradition, offering the first to the Mother, the Earth. You could use mulled wine and Christmas cookies as seasonal contributions for this ritual. Songs, stories, or poems that people may have brought can be shared here, and this is known as the *Gorsedd*. Before starting the ritual, establish who will take each role: North, South, East, West, Storyteller, Ritual Leader(s).

We close with each of the ritual elements in reverse order, unwinding the circle in the opposite direction to open the circle. People may like to remain by the fire afterward, chatting about the ritual, so you could end your ritual before the Gorsedd, spending longer afterward singing, drumming, and sharing stories, and poems. This *is* the Winter Solstice, however, and you may find yourselves chased inside by the cold.

A note about the songs: The Weaving song and the Yule song, which comes later, were both written specifically for this ritual and are available in a Forest Church music book and CD published by Ritualitas. (*Weaving The Sacred Circle* & *The Yule Log Song*, Words & Music: Alison Eve, copyright © 2012 Ritualitas. *The Year's Wheel Is Turning*, Melody:

Noel Nouvelet, traditional French Carol, Words: Alison Eve, Copyright © 2012 Ritualitas; this song has a verse for each of the eight seasons of the year.)

THE RITUAL

(Within the following activity, *italicized text* is to be spoken by the leader.)

> *The wheel of the year turns, spiraling out of the dark. We gather to celebrate the Winter Solstice, where the longest night gives way to the returning light, as the Christ Light is born into the deepest darkness, signaling the start of another cycle of growth and possibility. We give thanks for the lessons of the dark, midwife of the Christ Light, and prepare ourselves for the birth of Light within. The circle is prepared. Let us make our way to weave our sacred space together.*

Participants walk to the ritual space. Silence is held for a time so that each may connect to the space.

Sacred space is woven. (Adapt the words that follow, with their references to specific plants and animals, to fit your location.)

> *O Eternal Being, present in leaf and stone, in all that crawls and walks this sacred land, we honor the web of life within which we have all been woven. Here in this place we honor muntjac, robin, and squirrel; magpie and owl, fox and badger, blue-tit and wood-pigeon. We honor the mighty cedar in whose shade we meet, with evergreen, holly, fir, laurel, and ivy. And the ancient sentinel yew which stands at the gates of this place. We honor all those who have gone before us, who have stood where we stand now, waiting as the sun hangs unmoving in the southern sky, looking for the return of the light to the north, whose*

feasting, celebrating, and merriment still swell our hearts, whose songs sung to lighten the darkest and longest nights still resound in our memories and our souls. To all our ancestors of blood, land, and spiritual heritage,whether a handful of years or a thousand since gone, to all who gather here in peace, seen or unseen: We bid you hail and welcome!

All: *Hail and welcome!*

Spirit to spirit, heart to heart, leaf to leaf, root to root, we all share in the Divine Image.

Weaving and Consecrating the Circle

We weave our circle in the name of the Christ of Peace, drawing a calm about us, an encircling grace. We weave in the name of the Three of Grace, honoring the three world—sky, earth, and sea. We call for peace in this circle and throughout all the worlds.

While the following is sung, the ritual leader weaves the circle sunwise. Children can follow with light tinkling bells or sleigh bells as a metaphor of the protective circle of light. Each participant must help in this weaving by imagining this circle for themselves in some way.

We're weaving our sacred circle,
Weaving our temple of light,
We're weaving our sacred circle
In the name of the Christ of Peace. (repeat twice)

Christ with us, above and beneath us,
Christ all around us, Christ within. (repeat twice)

East: Carry incense sunwise around the inside of the circle, wafting it over each person.

We're weaving our sacred circle,
Weaving our temple of light,
We're weaving our sacred circle
In the name of the Three of Grace. (repeat twice)

Father of the sky and Son of the earth and Spirit of the
*   waters,*
Be with us. (repeat twice)

West: Carry the water sunwise around the inside of the circle, sprinkling each person.

We're weaving our sacred circle,
Weaving our temple of light,
We're weaving our sacred circle
In the name of the Christ of Peace. (repeat twice)

Peace in the north and peace in the south, peace in the east
and peace in the west. (repeat twice)

We're weaving our sacred circle,
Weaving our temple of light,
We're weaving our sacred circle
In the name of Christ.

Calling the Quarters

All turn to face each direction as it is called.

North:
O Holy Womb of Earth,
Holding the Christ Light within us all,
Nurturing and incubating heaven's seed
Through the long dark of winter.
We welcome the blessings of the north.
Hail and welcome!

All: *Hail and welcome!*

West:
> O Holy Well of Living Waters,
> Channeling the floods of birth and blood
> That herald the coming of the Christ Light
> At the moment of deepest darkness.
> We welcome the blessings of the west.
> Hail and welcome!

All: *Hail and welcome!*

South:
> O Holy Pillar of Sacred Fire
> Kindling and transforming our hearts
> As Light breaks through the darkness
> At the birthing of the Christ.
> We welcome the blessings of the south.
> Hail and welcome!

All: *Hail and welcome!*

East:
> O Holy Breath of wind and air,
> The sudden shocked inhalation of a newborn,
> At the birth of the Christ Light,
> A tiny warm cough in the midst of winter's freezing winds.
> We welcome the blessings of the east.
> Hail and welcome!

All: *Hail and welcome!*

> In silence we breathe the nine breaths of inspiration, mind-
> fully clearing our hearts and spirits of distractions and

busyness. Enter fully your bodies and this sacred space connecting with the presence of Spirit and Life all around.

Silence is kept.

The Blessings of the Dark

Between Samhain and Winter Solstice we seek to redress the imbalance that our spiritual tradition has historically created between light and dark, to honor the power and grace of the dark and winter. We plant the seeds of our hopes and dreams for the next cycle of growth into the cauldron of the Crone of Winter, the cauldron of rebirth, to take root in the long dark of winter.

Take the opportunity now to come again to the cauldron and place your hands into its depths, symbolically planting or reaffirming those seeds.

The ritual leader walks around the circle with the cauldron.

We are halfway through this time of waiting, of stillness, emptying, and darkness. Let us take a while to think of those things held safely and tenderly in the nurturing dark of the cauldron, the deep earth of the mother's heart.

Silence is kept.

O Mother, ground of all being, we give thanks to you for the nurturing depths of your heart. For the power of darkness to reshape and remake the world. O harsh and ruthless teacher, midwife of light and love and possibility, we give thanks for the courage and strength you wrench from deep within us in the dark cycle of our lives.

For fears to be faced and monsters befriended, for the lessons of solitude and rest, where we must come to terms with the true self without deceit or delusion or judgment. For bringing us safely to the deepest inner moment of the year, the center of the spiral where we discover the Christ Light ever burning within.

We bring our thanks offerings of food and place them on the Yuletide altar.

Yule Log

The fire is kindled and the Yule Log laid on it to burn. The Yuletide song is sung. There may be drumming at this point.

The long dark, the long nights,
The sun hangs low in the southern sky,
The wind blows, the frost bites,
The west is waiting with a watchful eye.

Come gather evergreen and mistletoe,
With holly hung above your door.
We'll wish you peace, health, and prosperity
With all the new year has in store.
Come gather wood to kindle up the fire
And put the Yule Log in the flame.
With cake and wine we'll feast and celebrate
The Light returning once again.

The long dark, the long nights,
The sun is gone from the northern sky,
The wind blows, the frost bites,
The east is waiting with a longing sigh.
Come gather acorns, myrrh, and frankincense
With an ivy crown upon your head.

We'll wish you honor, strength, and clarity
With all the passing year has shed.

Come gather wood to kindle up the fire
And put the Yule Log in the flame.
With cake and wine we'll feast and celebrate
The Light returning once again.

Storytelling: *Muime Chriosd*

At the turning of the wheel out of the dark cycle of stillness and silence, we listen to a story of the birth of the Light of the World.

Pronunciation guide:

Brighid *(Bree-yid)*
Muime Chriosd *(Mwee-mer Kree-osht)*: Foster-Mother of Christ
Fomhoire *(For-ver-rer)*
Tuatha Dé Danan *(Twa-tha Jay Da-nan)*
Dughal Donn *(Doo-gal Don)*
Sidhe *(Shee)*

Storyteller:

Come listen to my tale of Brighid, or Muime Chriosd, Foster-Mother of Christ, as she is known in Alba. It begins with Ireland in a time before time, where the Fomhoire held the world in violence and chaos. The Tuatha Dé Danan, with the goddess Brighid, wanted to bring the land to completion in beauty, and they labored together to make it so. As a last act, Brighid threw her green mantle over the world so that it became the beautiful green world we see today. She tied a knot in the cloak so it would not fall off the world—some say this knot is Tara Hill in Ireland.

Come travel with me now as the centuries spiral ever onward in time, until we reach again to Ireland, some 2000 years ago, where—ah, the scandal and the shame—a young princess is found to be with child! The only man close to her is the faithful servant, Dughal Donn. The princess brings a baby girl into the world and names her Brighid, but they are soon torn asunder, for the child and Dughal are exiled to avoid further dishonor to the clan.

Pushed out to sea in nothing but a coracle, a wee boat made of animal hide stretched over a wooden frame, they are sent away from Ireland out upon the open seas. For nine days they travel across the water in their upended drum. Eventually the currents carry them to a sacred wee island of Alba, Scotland, the Isle of Iona.

The druids there see the great potential and destiny laid on the girl and agree to offer them both shelter, with one strict condition—that the girl must be taught neither by man or by woman, but only by nature and the forces of the elements; nature's own wisdom would be her sole tutor.

Accepting this offer, Dughal and Brighid begin their new life on Iona. And so Brighid studies the natural world, learning the lessons of the elements. In time she grows into a beautiful and wise young woman.

But, kept apart from the druids, their teachings and rituals, Brighid becomes ever more curious about them. So, one midwinter's eve, under cover of darkness, she creeps up to the sacred hill used by the druids for their rites, and hides by the well of youth so that she may observe them in their dawn ritual.

Sometime later, she is awakened by the pitiful bleating of a newborn lamb in distress. Born too early, the lamb is now facing certain doom by a hungry hawk, poised to take advantage of the weakling. From inside her breaking heart Brighid wishes, as surely every sentient being must wish, that there could be a different law of life in the world, a law of love instead of blood. Her prayer is heard and two angels—or they might have been the Sidhe, maybe even a couple of the Tuatha Dé Danan—two great beings of light appear before her. They declare the coming birth of the Light of the World and ask for her help with this birth, telling her that it is her destiny to be midwife and foster-mother to the coming Light.

Readily accepting, Brighid is carried by the angels far, far away from Iona, across the world, to a cave where she finds the Mother beginning her labor. Throughout the long dark night, Brighid sits with the Mother in her labor, helping and encouraging her. Then, as the dawn breaks, the Light of the World is born. Brighid helps the child issue his first coughing breath and soothes him as he cries at the shock of it all. Brighid places the baby into the weary arms of the Mother.

After a time, the Mother sleeps, weary and exhausted, and Brighid holds the baby. She who has known nothing except the natural world of the elements sings a lullaby to the King of the Elements whom she holds in her arms.

(Someone starts singing the chant "Ha Meesh." After a while, continue over the top of this quiet song.)

Brighid tends to the baby, feeding him with the milk which spontaneously issues from her own virgin breast. Remembering her namesake, the goddess Brighid, she wraps the little king in her blue mantle, tying a knot in it so that it will not fall off—some say that knot is Iona. For forty days and nights she remains with the Mother and the King, nursing, helping, caring, and singing. (The chant ends.)

Then Brighid awakens to find herself back on Iona. But it is dark and so an Oyster catcher, also known as a Ghillie Brighid, a servant of Brighid, guides her back down the dark paths of the druid's sacred hill with its haunting cry.

She is guided straight to the druids and tells them all that has happened; she tells them of the birth of Light into the world.

Some recognize this as the great destiny they believed was in store for her when first she and Dughal came to Iona. Others, however, are not so convinced by what they regard as a fanciful tale. So Brighid puts her hand to her heart, drawing forth the Light from within, saying—"Look!" They look and see and know that it is so, the Light of the World has come.

The storyteller's candle is lit.

Thus begins her journey, which continues to the end of time and history across the trackways of the world, kindling the longing flame in the hearts of those she meets, the Light of the World, come to dwell in our hearts.

Each participant holds a candle lit from the storyteller's candle, while singing the following chant to the tune "Love Is Come Again."

The year's wheel is turning ever on its way,
From the dark emerging brighter every day.
Into the dark, where sleeps the sacred grain,
On the wings of morning, Light is born again.

Sharing the Feast

The wine and cake is blessed and the first portion given to our Mother. The wine and cake are shared around the circle with the words:

Drink that none may be thirsty, eat that none may go hungry.

Closing

Let us hold in our hearts the blessings of this ritual, that they may stay with us as we spiral slowly out of the dark winter, toward Imbolc and the start of spring. Let the seed of heaven in our hearts be brought to full term so that the light and peace of Christ may shine forth from within.

East:

Holy breath of life, we thank you for the chill winds that blow through us, making ready the path of the one who comes. Spirit of the East, thank you for being with us today. We bid you hail and farewell!

All: *Hail and farewell!*

South:

Holy and eternal fire, we thank you for the light that shines on a people who dwell in darkness. Spirit of the South, thank you for being with us today. Hail and farewell!

All: *Hail and farewell!*

West:

Holy well of living water, we thank you for the icy floods clearing the way of the one who comes. Spirit of the West, thank you for being with us today. We bid you hail and farewell!

All: *Hail and farewell!*

North:

Holy womb of earth, we thank you for the rebirth of light in a land of darkness. Spirit of the North, we thank you for being with us today. We bid you hail and farewell!

All: *Hail and farewell!*

We honor and give thanks for our ancestors of blood, land, and spiritual heritage for the blessings that resonate in our hearts. We bid you hail and farewell!

All: *Hail and farewell!*

We honor and give thanks for the hospitality of this place, for the web and energy of Life here, in muntjac and robin and owl and fox, for the mighty cedar who has watched over our ritual this Solstice. We bid you hail and farewell!

All: *Hail and farewell!*

Let the circle be opened that these blessings may be shared throughout the world.

The ritual leader unwinds the circle, walking moonwise three times.

Our celebration ends in peace as in peace it began. Peace without and peace within until we meet again. In the name of the Three of Grace, So may it be!

All: *So may it be!*

Further Resources

In the book references that follow, subtitles have been included only if the title of the book doesn't clearly describe the contents. Fifteen titles have been given an asterisk* to indicate that they would form a good starting reference library.

Chapter 1: Why Go Outside?

The Food Story and the Sacred Land: Colin Tudge, *So Shall We Reap* (Penguin, 2004). Toby Hemenway, *Gaia's Garden, Second Edition: A Guide to Home-Scale Permaculture* (Chelsea Green, 2011).

Nature Deficit Disorder: Richard Louv, *Last Child in the Woods* (Atlantic Books, 2010); *The Nature Principle** (Algonquin Books, 2012).

Flow: Mihaly Csikszentmihalyi, *Flow* (Rider, 2002).

Brain Waves: Anna Wise, *Awakening the Mind* (Jeremy P. Tarcher, 2002).

Chapter 2: Reading the Second Book of God

Awe: Alister McGrath, *The Re-enchantment of Nature** (Hodder & Stoughton, 2003).

Study: North American-biased resources by subject. I apologize that this list very much reflects my own interests (foraging carries the motivation of the Study subject being edible and leaves out an awful lot of other wonderful Study subjects (such as butterflies, which aren't edible).

Wild Flowers: The National Audubon Society has two excellent field guides, one for Eastern and one for Western wildflowers* (Knopf, 2001). Jack Sanders, *The Secrets of Wildflowers: A Delightful Feast of Little-Known Facts, Folklore, and History* (Lyons Press, 2010). Alexander C. Martin, *Weeds* (St. Martin, 2001).

Trees: Again, the National Audubon Society has two excellent field guides, one for Eastern and one for Western trees* (Knopf, 1980). Eric Rutkow, *American Canopy: Trees, Forests, and the Making of a Nation* (Scribner, 2012), and Donald Culross Peattie, *A Natural History of North American Trees* (Houghton Mifflin Harcourt, 2007); both these books contain the various trees' connections to American history as well as more scientific information regarding the species. Nancy R. Hugo, *Seeing Trees: Discover the Extraordinary Secrets of Everyday Trees* (Timber Press, 2001); invites you to "see" trees, not just identify them.

Mushrooms: Once again, I'd stick with the National Audubon Society's field guide (Knopf, 1981).

Birds, Insects, Mammals, Amphibians: So many books to choose from! You really need to find your own favorite. The National Audubon Society's field guides are excellent in any category.

Foraging: Ellen Zachos, *Backyard Foraging** (Storey, 2013). Samuel Thayer, *The Forager's Harvest: A Guide to Identifying, Harvesting, and Preparing Edible Wild Plants* (Forager's Harvest Press, 2006). John Kallas, *Edible Wild Plants* (Gibbs Smith, 2010).

Herbal Medicine: Alma R. Hutchens, *Indian Herbalogy of North America** (Shambhala, 2012). Charles W. Kane, *Herbal Medicine: Trends and Traditions* (Lincoln Tower, 2009). Jim Meuninck, *Medicinal Plants of North America: A Field Guide* (FalconGuides, 2008).

Permaculture: Aranya, *Permaculture Design* (Permanent Publications, 2012). Christopher Shein, *The Vegetable Gardener's Guide to Permaculture* (Timber, 2013).

Forest Gardening: Martin Crawford, *Creating a Forest Garden* (Green Books, 2010), *How to Grow Perennial Vegetables* (Green Books, 2012). Dave Jacke and Eric Toensmeier, *Edible Forest Gardens: Vol. 1 & 2* (Chelsea Green, 2006).

Bird Language: Jon Young, *What the Robin Knows* (Houghton Mifflin, 2012).

Natural Navigation: Tristan Gooley, *The Natural Navigator* (Experiment, 2012).

Tracking: Paul Rezendes, *Tracking and the Art of Seeing: How to Read Animal Tracks and Sign* (Collins, 1999).

Wilderness Survival: Nessmuk, *Woodcraft and Camping* (Cornerstone, 2013 reprint). Stackpole Books' *Survival Wisdom & Know How: Everything You Need to Know to Thrive in the Wilderness* (Black Dog & Leventhal, 2012).

Landscape Reading: Patrick Whitefield, *The Living Landscape** (Permanent Publications, 2010). Tom Wessels, *Reading the Forested Landscape* (Countryman, 2005). Ron Morton, *Talking Rocks: Geology and 10,000 Years of Native American Tradition* (University of Minnesota, 2003); combines geology with First Nation cultural tradition. A good introduction to geology is: Ron Redfern, *Making of a Continent* (Three Rivers Press, 1986). For a better understanding of place names across North America, there are numerous volumes that focus on specific regional areas.

Sacred Landscape: Belden C. Lane, *Landscapes of the Sacred** (Johns Hopkins, 2001). David Chidester and Edward T. Linenthal (editors), *American Sacred Space* (Indiana University Press, 1995). Keith H. Basso, *Wisdom Sits in Places: Landscape and Language Among the Western Apache* (University of New Mexico Press, 1996). Christopher P.

Scheitle, *Places of Faith: A Road Trip Across America's Religious Landscape* (Oxford University Press, 2012).

Biodiversity: Ken Thompson, *Do We Need Pandas?** (Green Books, 2011).

Ecosystem Services and Natural Capital: Tony Juniper, *What Has Nature Ever Done for Us?* (Profile Books, 2013).

Eco-psychology/Therapy: Michael J. Cohen, *Reconnecting with Nature* (Ecopress, 2007). Bill Plotkin, *Soulcraft* (New World Library, 2010), *Nature and the Human Soul* (New World Library, 2010). James Endredy, *Earthwalks for Body and Spirit: Exercises to Restore Our Sacred Bond with the Earth* (Bear & Company, 2002).

New Spiritualities: Graham Harvey, *Listening People, Speaking Earth: Contemporary Paganism* * (NYU Press, 2000).

Meaning and Natural Theology: Alister E. McGrath, *The Open Secret: A New Vision for Natural Theology* (Wiley-Blackwell, 2011). Jurgen Moltmann, *God in Creation* (Fortress, 1984); available mostly through used bookstores. A decent example of meaning-making is: Annie Heppenstall-West, *Reclaiming the Sealskin: Meditations in the Celtic Spirit* (Wild Goose Publications, 2004). Christine Valters Paintner, *Water, Wind, Earth, and Fire: The Christian Practice of Praying with the Elements* (Ave Maria Press, 2010). Graham B. Usher, *Places of Enchantment: Meeting God in Landscapes* (SPCK, 2012).

Chapter 4: Developing Your Wild Side

See above for resources already listed in the Study section.

Sit Spot & Nature Connection: Jon Young et al., *Coyote's Guide to Connecting with Nature** (Owlink Media, 2010), aimed at mentors of young people's outside activities, this book is packed with lots of activities and ideas. The Sit Spot exercise is covered in more detail in the context of bird language in: Jon Young, *What the Robin Knows* (Houghton Mifflin, 2012).

Going Out on Your Own and Wild Camping: Robert Macfarlane, *The Wild Places* (Penguin, 2008). Not a "how-to," (and written about the author's treks in the British Isles rather than North America) but quite inspirational, albeit from the perspective of *going into,* rather than *participating with* nature. Other titles by this writer are also well worth a read.

Pilgrimage: Dr. Sheryl A. Kujawa-Holbrook, *Pilgrimage— The Sacred Art: Journey to the Center of the Heart* (Skylight Paths, 2013). Phil Cousineau, *The Art of Pilgrimage: The Seeker's Guide to Making Travel Sacred* (Conari, 2012)

Growing Your Own: Carol Klein, *Grow Your Own Vegetables** (Mitchell Beazley, 2010). Jennifer Kujawski, *The Week-by-Week Vegetable Gardener's Handbook* (Storey, 2011). Jo Whittingham, *Backyard Harvest* (DK, 2011). See also resources given for permaculture and forest gardening.

Conversing with Nature: Bill Plotkin, *Soulcraft* (New World Library, 2011).

Start a New Life: Rebecca Laughton, *Surviving and Thriving on the Land* (UIT Cambridge, 2008). John Seymour, *The Self-Sufficient Life and How to Live It* (DK, 2009). See also permaculture resources.

Chapter 5: Growing Your Own Branch of Forest Church

Facilitation Skills: Dale Hunter, *The Zen of Groups* (Da Capo, 1995); *The Art of Facilitation** (Random House, 2012).

Ideas and Inspiration for Activities: Jon Young et al., *Coyote's Guide to Connecting with Nature* (Owlink Media, 2010). James Endredy, *Earthwalks for Body and Spirit: Exercises to Restore Our Sacred Bond with the Earth* (Bear & Company, 2002). Joseph Bharat Cornell, *Sharing Nature with Children* (Dawn, 1999). Geoffrey McMullan, *Discover Nature Awareness* (CreateSpace, 2012). Rob Cowen, Leo Critchley, *Skimming Stones and Other Ways* *of Being in the Wild* (Coronet, 2012). Tess Ward, *Celtic Wheel of the Year: Wild Celtic and Christian Seasonal Prayers* (Circle Books, 2007). Christine Valters Paintner, *Water, Wind, Earth, and Fire: The Christian Practice of Praying with the Elements* (Ave Maria Press, 2010).

Further resources for Forest Church and for nature connection for individuals are planned for the near future. Please visit www.forestchurch.co.uk to follow the news.

In the UK, those of us facilitating Forest Churches are planning to gather once or twice a year to camp together somewhere among beautiful nature and share stories, rituals, and activities. Join us if you can—but I encourage you to add your North American branches to the Forest Church tree. If you have decided to start your own branch of Forest Church, please get in contact so that we can list it on the website.

I am also available to give talks, workshops, retreats and courses on the subjects explored in this book and on nature-based spiritual direction. Contact me via www.embody.co.uk. For more information: www.forestchurch.co.uk or www.facebook.com/groups/forestchurch.

**The Mystic Path
of Meditation:
Beginning a
Christ-Centered Journey**
Author: David Cole
Price: $14.95 | UK £8.99
Paperback
Ebook Available
154 pages
ISBN: 978-1-937211-86-8

Explore the Christian theology that underpins meditation-and discover the practical spiritual benefits of this ancient practice.

"Meditation is one of the great treasures of our Christian contemplative tradition, though largely forgotten by modern churches. In this delightful book, David Cole gently invites readers to rediscover this ancient path to deeper relationship with God. David writes with a spirit of ease and joy as he guides us through meditation with scripture, our breath, our bodies, and the natural world. This insightful and accessible book is a welcome addition to the contemplative renewal of our time."

—Mark Kutolowski, OblSB, Salva Terra peace pilgrim and founder of New Creation Wilderness Programs

ANAMCHARA BOOKS
BOOKS TO INSPIRE
YOUR SPIRITUAL JOURNEY

In Celtic Christianity, an *anamchara* is a soul friend, a companion and mentor (often across the miles and the years) on the spiritual journey. Soul friendship entails a commitment to both accept and challenge, to reach across all divisions in a search for the wisdom and truth at the heart of our lives.

At Anamchara Books, we are committed to creating a community of soul friends by publishing books that lead us into deeper relationships with God, the Earth, and each other. These books connect us with the great mystics of the past, as well as with more modern spiritual thinkers. They are designed to build bridges, shaping an inclusive spirituality where we all can grow.

You can order our books at **www.AnamcharaBooks.com**. Check out our site to read opinions and perspectives from our editorial staff on our Soul Friends blog. You can also submit your own blog posts by emailing **info@AnamcharaBooks. com** with "Blog Entry for Soul Friends" in the subject line. To find out more about Anamchara Books and connect with others on their own spiritual journeys, visit **www.AnamcharaBooks. com** today.

ANAMCHARA BOOKS
220 Front Street
Vestal, New York 13850
(607) 785-1578
www.AnamcharaBooks.com

CPSIA information can be obtained at www.ICGtesting.com
Printed in the USA
BVOW03s0959260514

354490BV00001B/7/P